# Michael H. Zurfluh

# The Truth About Money

**A Common Sense Approach to a Debt-Free Life**

Copyright © 2013 by Michael H. Zurfluh

All rights reserved, including the right of reproduction in whole or in any part or form. No portion of this book may be reproduced, stored in a retrieval system, or transmitted in any form or by any means—electronic, mechanical, photocopy, recording, scanning, or other—except for brief quotations in critical reviews or articles, without the prior written consent of the publisher.

Published in Stevens Point, Wisconsin by Michael H. Zurfluh.

For information about bulk purchases, please contact Michael Zurfluh at getzurf@gmail.com.

Cover Design Copyright © 2013 by Working Class Publishing, Stevens Point WI.
www.workingclasspublishing.com

**Library of Congress Cataloging-in-Publication Data**

Zurfluh, Michael H.
The Truth About Money: A Common Sense Approach to a Debt Free Life
ISBN 978-0-615-845258

Library of Congress Control Number: 2013914480

Manufactured in the United States of America

10 9 8 7 6 5 4 3 2 1

*For My Family*

My sisters, Ramona (Moe), Chris, Sue, Mary Jane, Cindy, Ann, and my brother Dave: You are the best family I could have ever asked for. Thanks for all your support and listening and help over the years.

My mother, Honey: As I stated in your eulogy, you were, are, and always will be the biggest influence in my life. You are my hero—I love you Mom.

My wife, Celeste: Thanks for all your support over the years. You made me believe in myself even when I didn't. I love you.

My daughters, Sadie Ramona Zurfluh and Macie Rita Zurfluh: You are the best thing that has ever happened to me. How come I love you so much? Because I do! Love Dad.

*Attitude Determines Altitude.*

*unknown*

# Table of Contents

Introduction vii

1. My Early Years 1
2. Zurf's and K.I.S.S 15
3. The Power of Compounding Interest: Positive and Negative 21
4. Saving for Financial Freedom 31
5. Learn What You Do Now Affects You Tomorrow 47
6. Do You Really Need That Stuff? 63
7. Credit Is Not Your Friend 79
8. Budget 89
9. Marriage 105
10. Assets 113
11. Spending Habits 125
12. Financial Goals and Retirement Planning 135
13. Just Ask 139
14. Real Estate Investments 151
15. Kids/ Education 175
16. Cash Is King 187
17. Giving Back 193
18. Closing 197

*A wise man should have money in his head, but not in his heart.*

Jonathan Swift

# Introduction

Today is April 29. I have been talking about writing a book for years and this is the day that I finally start.

My name is Michael Harold Zurfluh, but I prefer to be called Mike or Zurf. While I know that is not important to this book, I want my readers to know that I am just an ordinary man, a man with a plan for my life. My plan is to live life to the fullest and enjoy every day.

Someone once said "Money can't buy you happiness." While I believe that statement is true, let me tell you that not having money or being in financial trouble can lead your life in an unhappy and stressful direction.

My goal in writing this book is to help those who read it attain financial freedom. For most people there is way too much month left at the end of the money. Living paycheck to paycheck is not the way to live a full life. I have read hundreds of books in my life, many of them on real estate and creating wealth. While I have made my money in real estate, this book will focus more on teaching you how to plan for financial freedom and forming GREAT spending and saving HABITS.

Yesterday, I became a grandfather for the first time. This is scary as I look at my grandson and his mother and father, and fear for the struggles they will encounter. Adversity can make people stronger, yet the world we live in today makes it very easy to get into financial difficulties.

Most people who buy this book will not read it. You have taken the first step. I will do my best to keep it interesting with stories from my life and of others that have interacted in my life.

**Have a Super Fantastic Life.** Have a Super Fantastic Life.

Money is better than poverty, if only for financial reasons.

                                                         Woody Allen

# My Early Years

I was born on Feb 10, 1961 to Ramona (Honey) Zurfluh and Harold Zurfluh. Like Bob Yuker once said, on the ride home from the hospital, they stopped at the grocery store and bought me some beef jerky to toughen me up for the Cinderella story that was about to begin.

At the age of 8, my father died following a sudden heart attack. I was the youngest of eight children and my father had been a hard worker all his life. He worked in the paper mill and took extra jobs to get ahead in life. He needed to take care of his big family. While he didn't leave our family wealthy, there was some money in the bank and he didn't leave us with debt. He had financial dealings that my mother understood, and would continue to help us for years to come.

I was fortunate enough to have a mother who saved, one who was very frugal but not cheap. The difference between frugal and cheap: Frugal is clipping coupons and looking for the deals. Cheap is not chipping in for gas with your friends or not taking your turn to buy a round of drinks. Her habits have impacted my life in a very positive way.

At 10 years old, I began doing yard work for neighbors and relatives to earn money. By 16, I was working at a

*Unlock your potential: The possibility for expansion and growth is inside us all.*

*— unknown*

restaurant and a sporting goods store and had purchased my first car and motorcycle. I also paid for the insurance and upkeep myself. Even though I spent money, I was still always putting some money away in my savings account. When I graduated from high school, like most kids I was unsure what I wanted to do. I began my pursuit of a Police Science degree but during the first semester I realized that was not the career for me. Searching for a different direction, I completed a one-year degree in Wood Technics. Unbeknown to me at the time, this one-year program proved to be very valuable as it taught me how to build and repair homes.

Right before my father died, I watched Neil Armstrong land on the moon. I remember sitting on the couch with my father and he kept waking me up, saying I shouldn't miss such an important event in history. Ever since then, I had been interested in flying. Thinking this was my destiny, I decided to get my pilot's license and I began to pursue a professional career in aviation. I was accepted into an aviation school in Missouri and planned to start school in August, 1981.

But on July 19, 1981 my life was changed forever. While leaving my summer job at the paper mill on my motorcycle, a truck came out of the parking lot and smashed into me. I still remember this like it was yesterday, and remember flying through the air in slow motion, wishing I had put my helmet on.

As I landed, time returned to normal, and I checked to see if I could move my hands and my left leg. I knew immediately there was something wrong with my right leg. As I positioned my body, I could see a bone sticking out of my leg. Emergency surgery was needed and I spent 11 months in a cast. I know what you're thinking: I got a BIG insurance settlement out of this accident. I only wish that was the case. The guy who hit me had a $15,000 insur-

**Have a Super Fantastic Life.** Have a Super Fantastic Life.

*When you stop to think, don't forget to start again.*

— *unknown*

ance policy. The insurance company forfeited the $15,000 after an attorney talked me into signing with them. After all was said and done, the attorney got one-third, workers' comp got one-third, and I ended up with one-third. $5000: NOT A LOT OF MONEY.

To this day I still have difficulty with my right leg. I've had three surgeries since the accident and the current recommendation is for me to have my leg re-broken, a rod put in, and then a total knee replacement when it heals. While I could look at this as a tragedy, I choose to look at this adversity as a blessing in disguise. The realization of how short life really is became very evident. The accident and 11 months in a cast changed my personality. I had been a little shy, but afterwards realized being shy wasn't going to help me get what I wanted. I needed to speak up.

One example of my insecurity was when it came to girls in high school. There was one girl I wanted to ask out, but I would only call her home and hang up when someone answered (obviously before the days of caller ID). Finally, after more than two months of working up the courage, I asked her out on a date. We did end up going to Homecoming together but I still didn't have much confidence. After two dates, I quit calling her. When I look back on those days, I really never had any serious relationships or very many dates. My approach to life changed after the accident, including my approach to dating girls. I had more confidence to ask girls out. I would be out at a local nightclub and see a girl I was attracted to. Before my accident, I would just look at her and think, "Boy, is she pretty." After my accident, I had the confidence to approach those girls and ask them if they wanted a drink or to dance. Even rejections no longer bothered me. I remember one time I asked a girl to dance and she said "No." I responded, "That's fine, I was just kidding anyway." Later that night she came up to me and asked me to dance, yes I danced with her.

**Have a Super Fantastic Life.**

*YOU MUST BELIEVE TO ACHIEVE!*

*unknown*

My self-confidence was not dependent on how a girl responded. The accident made me realize how short life really is and how it can change in a BLINK. The accident, while a tragedy, was in some ways also a blessing. My self-confidence soared after the accident. It made me realize that no one is better than anyone else. It is just our confidence level that makes us all different.

You don't need a tragedy to make these types of changes in your life. You can act now and change for the better.

After my leg injury and subsequent disability, I realized a career in aviation may not be the best. Instead of aviation I attained an Associate Degree in Marketing and Real Estate.

I bought my first house in 1982. A friend of mine offered me $100. I asked, "What for?" He said, "To send you to a psychologist." The house was a one-bedroom home that six people lived in. It was disgusting, to say the least, but I saw potential.

I fixed the home up on my own, rented it out for a positive monthly cash flow, and sold it a couple years later for a $7,000 profit. I borrowed the money from my mother for my first home. I typed up the agreement and we both signed it. I paid her more than she was getting on her savings account and less than I would have had to pay with a bank loan. It was a win-win. When I rented it out I moved back home with my mother and paid her rent until I bought Zurf's.

I continued to buy some real estate (buying real estate will be discussed in later chapters) and then opened a bar and restaurant in 1983 (Zurf's For the Good Times). The building was previously a bar and restaurant, but when I bought the place it was vacant and in shambles. I used the profit I made from selling that first house to buy others and for the down payment on Zurf's. Many of the properties I bought with no money down. This is also discussed more in later chapters.

**Have a Super Fantastic Life.** Have a Super Fantastic Life.

Q: Who has pain?
A: Everyone.

Q: What are they looking for?
A: A cure.

Q: How do you find your niche in life?
A: Identify the pain and suggest the cure.

unknown

For Zurf's, I made two offers to the owner who lived in Las Vegas. The first offer was for the full asking price with a list of seller credits (money the seller would give back at closing for windows, carpet, etc.) for all the work that needed to be done. I took the time (a lot of time) to get estimates for everything that needed to be fixed. I believe he was asking $129,900 for this property back in 1983. I also made a second offer to him at the same time for $65,000. Both offers included him giving me a land contract. The purpose of the first offer was to show him all the work that needed to be done. We closed on the second offer with me taking the property as is and him giving me a land contract for $65,000. I gave $10,000 as a down payment. The purchase price was $75,000. I sold my pickup truck and other things to come up with the $10,000. I bought a beater truck for $250 for transportation. I put everything I had into this.

I also needed money to use for repairs and start up. I borrowed $10,000 from a friend of mine. I still can't believe he did this. We hand wrote on a piece of paper Dean loans Zurf $10,000 at 7% interest to be paid back in two years and we both signed it. I paid him back in full with interest in less than a year. For the first two years I would stick most of the profits back into Zurf's, fixing it up and improving it along the way. I added a kitchen, volleyball courts, meeting room, and more.

For over 10 years, Zurf's occupied most of my time. I did real estate on a part time basis during those years, selling a few houses a year to friends and family. Then, once again adversity struck and led me to make changes. The real estate office I worked for decided not to have part time real estate agents. So instead of quitting real estate, I started my own office and joined the weekly broker/MLS meetings. At one of the meetings, another broker promoted a mobile home park. Having owned about six rental properties at the time, I had learned the benefits of positive cash flow (income of $700 with expense of $500 is $200 positive

*Your future is limited only by the size of your thoughts.*

— unknown

cash flow). While I scratched the numbers on my notebook during this meeting, I thought my math was wrong and couldn't believe the cash flow numbers of this property. After further calculation, I found the numbers to be accurate and I purchased my first mobile home park.

I had been one of those who believed mobile home parks harbored "trailer trash." I am a firm believer that when people live in a clean, neat environment, that the tenants will take pride in where they live. Trash breeds trash, cleanliness breeds cleanliness. That was my goal: to make positive changes to the mobile home park. I also required the tenants to make changes, and in doing so, made it a better place for everyone who lived there.

In September of 1994, I sold Zurf's and my real estate career began to soar. The day after the sale, I proposed to the Love of My Life, and she said "Yes."

One of my unaccomplished goals was to have a bachelor's degree (my mother had always dreamed this for me, too). With the support of my wife, I completed a business degree and graduated Magma Cum Laude from Lakeland College, Sheboygan, WI. On my graduation day, my sister gave me a graduation card. She told me to open it right before the graduation ceremony. The card contained a note and photo of my mom and dad. It said, "Carry this with you when you get your diploma as I know Mom and Dad would both be very proud of you and they will be there with you on your special day." My mother had died on December 15, 1997, just 5 months before I graduated from college. I was 37 at the time.

Achieving my degree was something not only my parents had wanted for me, but was a personal goal that I had. What was more important than the piece of paper I obtained that day was the knowledge I gained along the way. Knowledge that has benefited me numerous times and will continue to benefit me in the future. Education is truly necessary on

**Have a Super Fantastic Life.** Have a Super Fantastic Life.

*The toughest thing to change about change is our attitude toward change.*

*unknown*

the path to success in life. Ignorance is the fate of one too lazy to be intelligent.

Over the next 15 years, I continued to list and sell real estate. I have been the top producing Realtor in our market since 1995. During this time, I purchased many properties, at one point owning six manufactured home parks for a total of over 400 rental units.

Now at the age of 49, I realize even more how short life really is, and have begun selling off properties that are higher maintenance and are more difficult to rent out. I am currently on a path to be debt free at 58 and have passive income (money you make when not working) from rental properties of over $25,000 per month.

> DON'T STOP READING. YOU DON'T HAVE TO HAVE RENTAL UNITS TO REACH FINANCIAL FREEDOM.

Looking back on what I would do differently if I could live my life over, it would be to save more money monthly, and place it in a tax deferred retirement account.

While I believe I will still have financial freedom, saving in this manner would have put me in a much better position. There is an old saying I have heard numerous times, "Pay Yourself First." The older I get, the more I understand this statement. Over the course of my career, I have dealt with an unbelievable number of people who make good money but don't have a pot to pee in or a window to throw it out of.

The following chapters will make a difference in your life and the lives of your family and friends. Remember: Attitude is Everything. My personal philosophy and my trademark statement at the end of many of my conversations is: "Have a Super Fantastic Day."

**Have a Super Fantastic Life.** Have a Super Fantastic Life.

> My goal in writing this book is to help you, the Reader, have a SUPER FANTASTIC LIFE, as I have had thus far. One of the primary means of accomplishing that kind of life is to attain financial freedom.
>
> Mike Zurfluh

**Have a Super Fantastic Life.** Have a Super Fantastic Life.

# 2 Zurf's and K.I.S.S.

This chapter is short to show the beauty of keeping things simple…

Most people are NEVER taught about money, NOT in school and NOT by their parents. This is part of the problem our world has with money.

I learned when I owned Zurf's that when buying any property or business you make your profit when you buy not when you sell.

When I was looking at the property which became Zurf's, I was also dealing on another property. Both the seller of that property and I became cemented on the price that she was willing to sell for and I was willing to pay. Neither of us gave in, and I did not purchase that property. It had all the potential I was looking for, including living quarters, room for a kitchen, outside volleyball, large enough to accommodate live bands and the location was better than the place I ended up buying.

She eventually lost that property to foreclosure, and although Zurf's did okay during my period of ownership, I know it would have done fantastic in the other location.

*The trouble with life is, you are halfway through before you realize it is one of those do-it-yourself deals.*

*unknown*

As you have probably heard before, there are three things in real estate that are important: Location, Location, Location. Had I known then what I know now, I would have continued to negotiate with this seller. I should have looked for other ways, out-of-the-box ways, to purchase the property with the better location. We were only $10,000 apart. At the time it seemed like a lot of money. What I should have done was agree to pay $10,000 more. I was willing to pay $100,000 and she wanted $110,000. I would have been buying it on a land contract. $100,000 at 7% over 20 years is $775.30 per month. $110,000 at 5.75% over 20 years is $772.29 per month. Looking back I am sure she would have agreed to this. It would have saved me $3.01 per month to give her $10,000 more if she would have gone with the lower interest rate. She would have gotten the price she wanted, and I would have been much more successful in that location. Plus, my payments would have been less than paying the price I wanted. The lesson is to find out what the goals of the selling party are. In this case hers was $110,000. I should have found a way to make that happen.

When my career with Zurf's was over, I learned that the way to be successful is NOT to try to please everyone. K.I.S.S. (Keep It Simple Stupid) is the way to be successful. When I started with Zurf's, we had a small menu with burgers and Friday Fish Fry. I made more money than I had dreamed of. My last year at Zurf's I had more than 25 employees, a five page menu and over $500,000 in sales, but Zurf's made no profit.

I could list a thousand things that I did wrong at Zurf's but I will give a couple of examples. When I first opened, I had a customer that asked for Jim Beam Rye so I bought three bottles (buy three get them at a discount). Ten years later when I sold Zurf's I had the same three bottles of Jim Beam Rye minus a few shots sold to that one customer. We had more potato choices than any place I have ever eaten

*THINK BIG— IT PAYS BETTER!!!*

*Mike Zurfluh*

at. We had homemade French fries, regular French fries, criss-cross French fries, baked potatoes, cheesy baked potatoes, sour cream baked potatoes, and potato salad. Seven different types of potatoes are way too many.

I created what I thought was my dream, making as many people happy as I could. But instead I created a monster. Had I kept it simple, I would have continued to keep the money rolling in.

If I had to do it over I would have been open at the most five days per week, maybe even three days. If it were three days it would be Thursday, Friday, and Saturday. Friday was a third of our business. I even opened for breakfast at 6:00 a.m. Being open three to five days would give down time for everyone, including our customers, who would've then wanted to come more on the days we were open. I would have kept my menu much smaller, featuring the best hamburgers in town, fresh homemade rolls, a Friday Fish Fry, and homemade pizza. I know this would have made Zurf's much more profitable.

Everyone has different dreams and that is what makes our world work. I have owned apartment buildings, duplexes, vacant land, storage units, commercial shopping centers, and commercial office space. By far the easiest and safest investments have been single family homes and senior manufactured home parks.

As I begin to reevaluate my life, my goal over the next seven years is to dispose of my properties that aren't single family and senior manufactured home parks. This will allow for great passive income and fewer headaches.

**Have a Super Fantastic Life.** Have a Super Fantastic Life.

*When you come to the financial fork in the road and you don't know where your goals are, it doesn't make any difference which way you go.*

*unknown*

# 3
# The Power of Compounding Interest: Positive and Negative

Albert Einstein was once asked to identify the most powerful invention he'd ever seen. His answer was COMPOUNDING INTEREST (earning interest on interest)!

Compounding interest can work to make you financially independent or can work to give you a life of financial misery.

To make this point more clear suppose I hired you to work for me for a month straight. Would you rather I paid you a penny a day, doubled for 31 days or $5,000.00 each day?

Answer this question before you turn the page.


$5,000.00 each day for 31 days is $155,000.00. That is a lot of money. However...


**Have a Super Fantastic Life.** Have a Super Fantastic Life.

*The art of waking up... How we program our minds in the first 3-5 minutes of our day... has a dramatic impact on the remaining 1,435 minutes of any particular day of our lives.*

*unknown*

# COMPOUNDING INTEREST

A penny a day doubled is:

| Day 1  | $0.02 |
| Day 2  | $0.04 |
| Day 3  | $0.08 |
| Day 4  | $0.16 |
| Day 5  | $0.32 |
| Day 6  | $0.64 |
| Day 7  | $1.28 |
| Day 8  | $2.56 |
| Day 9  | $5.12 |
| Day 10 | $10.24 |
| Day 11 | $20.48 |
| Day 12 | $40.96 |
| Day 13 | $81.92 |
| Day 14 | $163.84 |
| Day 15 | $327.68 |
| Day 16 | $655.36 |
| Day 17 | $1,310.72 |
| Day 18 | $2,621.44 |
| Day 19 | $5,242.88 |
| Day 20 | $10,971.52 |
| Day 21 | $20,971.52 |
| Day 22 | $41,943.04 |
| Day 23 | $83,886.08 |
| Day 24 | $167,772.16 |
| Day 25 | $335,544.32 |
| Day 26 | $671,088.64 |
| Day 27 | $1,342,177.28 |
| Day 28 | $2,684,354.56 |
| Day 29 | $5,368,709.12 |
| Day 30 | $10,737,418.24 |

The total for day 31 is **$21,474,836.48**

**Have a Super Fantastic Life.** Have a Super Fantastic Life.

> *Success is the sum of small efforts, repeated day in and day out.*
>
> — Robert Collier

So now, with the calculations completed, what would you prefer? No question, I want the penny a day, doubled for 31 days! Wow, this definitely shows the power of compounding interest. To give you an example of how normally compounding interest works: If you buy and finance $100,000 over 30 years at 6% interest and make the payments as scheduled for 30 years, you will be paying back $215,841.60. You will be paying more to the bank than you are for your house.

Another example is if you save $500 per month for 30 years at 6% interest, after 30 years you will have $502,257.52. You will have invested $180,000 of your own money but the compounding interest will have increased your $180,000 by $322,257.52.

Now you can see the beauty of compounding interest when saving money and how expensive compounding interest can be when you are borrowing money.

I wish I had understood compounding interest at a much younger age. If I would have realized this when I was 20, I would have been in a much better financial position today.

Later in this book I will teach you about tracking your money. I am sure everyone can find a way that they can save $2.00 a day. Whether it is not stopping for a cup of coffee, not going through the drive thru, or smoking fewer cigarettes, $2.00 a day can make a difference.

Saving $2.00 a day, invested at 7.25% interest for 65 years, gives you $1,010,815.74 in your pocket.

It's hard and it's not hard to save $2.00 a day. The best way to save $2.00 every day is to make it automatic. You can have it deducted from your paycheck and put into a savings plan or have it automatically moved into a savings plan from your checking account. The key is once it is in the designated savings you do not touch it for ANY reason!

**Have a Super Fantastic Life.** Have a Super Fantastic Life.

*There is no OFF switch on a Tiger!!*

*unknown*

## COMPOUNDING INTEREST

While I am not suggesting that you should physically put $2.00 into your savings each day, you can have $14.00 put in if you are paid weekly, or $28.00 if you are paid biweekly, or $62.00 if you are paid monthly. I know you are thinking $62.00 a month is a lot of money, but remember it is only $2.00 per day and I know you can find the $2.00 you spend each day. Then, you can start making YOUR million dollars. You have to start somewhere! Why not give it a try?

Here is the fun part. If you are married and you each save $2.00 per day, you can have a million dollars in 56 years.

If you are a smoker paying $7.50 for a pack of cigarettes, and you save that $7.50 per day, you will have a million dollars if invested at 7% for 47 years. If you are married and both of you smoke (and quit), saving $15 per day, you will have a million dollars in 37.5 years.

Another great way to assure your financial stability is investing in real estate.

You can purchase real estate with little or no money down. I have read hundreds of books on real estate and several that teach you how to buy a property and put money in your pocket. I am not sold on this idea as you are borrowing money from yourself that you have to pay back with interest. However, a great way to test the waters in real estate is to buy a duplex. Live in one half and rent out the other. I highly recommend side-by-side duplexes. The key is making your profit when you buy. Look for motivated sellers or properties that need some light fixing up.

The beauty of purchasing real estate is that you have a lower dollar amount investment, real estate appreciates and your renter pays the mortgage. For example: If you have $10,000 saved up and you invest with 10% return for one year, you now have $11,000. That is a $1000 profit. In real estate if you buy a property for $100,000 with 10% down, and that goes up 10% in a year, the value is now $110,000. Subtract the $10,000 you invested and the monthly rental

**Have a Super Fantastic Life.**

As I educated myself on human behavior and financial strategies, I learned that it's actually the people who make their money work hard for them, rather than the people who work hard for their money, who end up with more of it.

*unknown*

payment, which brings what you owe on the property to under $90,000. You will now have a profit of over $10,000. This is more than 100% return on your investment.

I typically buy properties with a positive cash flow that will pay themselves off in 15 to 20 years. For example: If I buy a home, and after improvements my payments (including principle, interest, taxes, and insurance) is $625.00 per month for 15 years, I want to make sure I can rent this property for a minimum of $700 per month.

Now let's look at negative compounding interest. There are several ways that compounding interest is a negative to you. Most notably: credit card debt when you don't pay your balance in full.

Credit cards when paid in full on a monthly basis do have some advantages. However, most people I know do not pay them in full or even look at their statements to verify that all their charges are correct. If you pay the minimum payment, you begin the treadmill of ruining your financial independence for years to come. Not only do you pay high interest, you also pay a monthly fee and the interest keeps compounding and compounding on the unpaid balance. For example: You owe $10,000 on your credit card and the interest rate is 18%. If you miss a payment you will have a late fee/penalty of (for example) $50. If you did not charge anything more for a month, next month you would owe the balance of $10,000, plus late fee/penalty of $50, plus the interest for two months of $150.00. The new balance you would owe would be $10,200. This would be $2400 over the course of a year. Need I say more? If you have credit cards, pay them in FULL every month or get rid of them.

Einstein defined insanity as doing the same thing over and over again and expecting different results.

Go to www.getzurf.com to access a financial calculator that can show you how to pay off debt or grow your money so you can become financially free.

**Have a Super Fantastic Life.** Have a Super Fantastic Life.

The best way I know to judge is this: You have to want it more than you want anything else in the world. And most important, you have to be sure you NEVER GET IT.

The successful people I know always have a carrot in front of them, slightly out of reach, no matter how many carrots they already have. When he was thirty, Lou Holtz wrote down a list of 107 lifetime ambitions on a slip of paper. They ranged from owning a 1949 Chevy to being invited to the white house for dinner. By the time he was fifty-two he had achieved eighty-six of them. Do you want to bet whether he'll make the other twenty-one? And when he does, if he'll tear up the list and write down another 107?

unknown

**Have a Super Fantastic Life.** Have a Super Fantastic Life.

# 4 Saving for Financial Freedom

Most Americans fail to save. Saving is crucial in order to achieve financial independence. Pennies saved can make the difference.

I watched a television show once where they put a penny on the sidewalk and observed to see how many people stopped and picked it up. It was very few. Then, they tried a nickel with similar results. Next it was a quarter, and more people, but not a lot of them, stopped and picked it up. Then they placed a one-dollar bill and almost all of the people walking by stopped to pick it up. This is probably the trouble with America, we think it is beneath us to pick up a penny. But one hundred pennies is a dollar, and that accumulation of pennies is what can lead to financial freedom. There is an old song called "Luther" by Boxcar Willie (hear it at www.getzurf.com):

> *Luther, here's a dollar*
> *Luther, here's a quarter*
> *Take either one you want, old man*
> *Which one will it be*
>
> *He lived and died in squalor*
> *And he still won't take the dollar*
> *But there's a pile of quarters*
> *Heaped high on Luther's grave*

**Have a Super Fantastic Life.** Have a Super Fantastic Life.

One of my favorite examples of the connection between thoughts and feelings is that of someone reading a magazine. Suppose you were reading a story about a little girl and her pony. Although she was only ten years old, she had been winning national contests for several years. You might think," Wow, that's really neat." If so, you'd probably be feeling uplifted, or even inspired.

On the other hand, you might think to yourself," What a spoiled brat. She must have rich parents." If you thought this instead, you would be feeling cynical. What's interesting is that the words on the page were exactly the same. They did not cause your emotion, your thoughts did.

unknown

# SAVING

The song ends with Luther saying that if he chose the dollar no one would offer him the choice anymore. He died with lots of quarters.

Saving $1.00 a day for 40 years is $78,744. As stated earlier, two people that smoke a pack a day and quit, saving $7.50 per pack, $15 per day at 7% interest for 40 years save $1,181,166.03

If you can save $10 per day ($3650 per year) or if married and both work $20 per day ($7300 per year) at 7% you would have a million dollars in:

$10 per day ---------------------------------------- 43 years

$20 per day---------------------------------------- 34 years

(In 34 years total it would be $1,014,741.05)

I know what you are saying: "Yeah, right. How am I going to save $3650/$7300 extra per year when I am living paycheck to paycheck now?"

It's not easy, but it is worth it. If you are making $10 per hour that is 31 extra hours per month per person. That breaks down to about 7.5 hours per week. Look for ways to cut costs, ask to work overtime, or get a part time job.

The 7.5 hours is if you are making $10 per hour. Most of you make more than that. Get a server job for Friday nights. 15 years ago on Friday nights my servers made about $20 per hour, most of which was cash. This was for about four to five hours work. We pay a cleaning lady $12 per hour cash. There are part time jobs that with only four extra hours per week (or less) you can save this amount. If you cut your expenses, you might even be able to save the money without extra work. But to get there faster cut expenses and work extra. I used to referee basketball games about 20 years ago, making around $30 to $40 per game.

The High School level is always looking for referees and is a good way to make extra money. I coach my daughters

**Have a Super Fantastic Life.** Have a Super Fantastic Life.

> Ideas belong to whoever can use them, not just the person who is first through the door of the patent office
>
> — Stephen Coonts

in junior high school basketball and I have seen the paychecks. Referees earn $30 per game, which last about one hour. They usually work two games in one night (seventh and eighth grade). It is a great way to make extra money and pay down debt or save for your financial independence.

> EVERYONE'S MINIMUM FINANCIAL GOALS SHOULD BE TO HAVE SAVED A MINIMUM OF ONE MILLION DOLLARS AND BE DEBT FREE AT TIME OF RETIREMENT.

Financial freedom means many things to many people. To me, financial freedom is when you have enough passive income to cover your normal day-to-day expenses for the rest of your life. Then, you are financially free.

My definition of passive income is revenue sources you have without working. Examples of this are: interest on a savings account, interest earned from stock investments, income from investment properties (such as rentals, commercial, or others), and income from renting out your vacation home or properties while you are not using them.

Too many people are slaves to the MONEY. Once you are debt free and have passive income exceeding your expenses, you will truly experience freedom.

Freedom is being able to choose what you do every day. Whether that is going to work, helping a friend, volunteering at a local organization, playing a round of golf, or spending time with your spouse, the bottom line is that you are totally in control of your choices in life.

Everyone's desires change as they grow older. Some people want more, some people are content with what they have, and some people want less. You and your spouse need to decide on your future and the goals you have to make it a GREAT one.

**Have a Super Fantastic Life.** Have a Super Fantastic Life.

*Experience is a mistake you live through.*

— Stephen Coonts

# SAVING

I joined Weight Watchers in October 2008 after I saw a friend of mine had lost weight and looked great. I asked her how she did it and she said by joining Weight Watchers. Several people asked me why I joined because I looked good, but I was not happy with how I looked or felt. I was up to 250 pounds (at 6'2" I was more than 50 pounds overweight). I dropped 30 pounds and I feel much better about myself. My goal now is to be between 200 and 210. As of today, I am 14 pounds within reaching my goal.

One of the benefits of Weight Watchers is a saying "if you bite it, write it." This helped me a lot, but what has helped me even more is to write it before I bite it. This helps me to remain focused and achieve my goals.

I believe the same is true about writing everything you spend. Whether it is putting a nickel in a parking meter, donating five dollars in the church collection, buying an ice cream cone, paying your utility bills, write it all down. At the end of the month, analyze how you are spending your money. Just by getting in the habit of writing it down, it may help change your spending habits. On the following page is a chart (you can print it at www.getzurf.com) for you to write down everything you spend in a month.

When you spend it, write it!

Use this chart for one month and write down EVERY penny you spend. Then look for ways you can save money. My guess is you will find more ways to save than you think.

**Have a Super Fantastic Life.**

Chase your dreams. Shout them to the world if you feel brave enough. And when you get discouraged, remember that only in wartime is failure fatal.

*unknown*

**SAVING**     **39**

| Date | ITEM PURCHASED | $ Spent | NEED | WANT |
|---|---|---|---|---|
| | | | | |
| | | | | |
| | | | | |
| | | | | |
| | | | | |
| | | | | |
| | | | | |
| | | | | |
| | | | | |
| | | | | |
| | | | | |
| | | | | |
| | | | | |
| | | | | |
| | | | | |
| | | | | |
| | | | | |
| | | | | |
| | | | | |
| | | | | |
| | | | | |

**Have a Super Fantastic Life.** Have a Super Fantastic Life.

When you are feeling at your lowest, go out and do something for someone worse off because the main goal in life is to raise up the lowest...

*unknown*

All the following items need to be listed on your worksheet. Make sure they are a need and not just a want.

| | | |
|---|---|---|
| Restaurant | Books | Real estate taxes |
| Insurance | Home insurance | Electric |
| Education | Auto insurance | Gas |
| Clothing | Health insurance | Phone |
| Recreation | Dental insurance | Water |
| Major purchases | Life insurance | Sewer |
| Vacation | Gas | Cable or satellite |
| Auto purchase | Auto expense | Bank charges |
| Furniture | House expense | Charity |
| Tuition | Groceries | Tithe |
| Room and board | Rent | |

What I noticed with Weight Watchers is that I used to eat more often, and more unhealthy foods. Now, I am eating less and am eating healthier.

The same is true with money, we all spend foolishly at times. Super-sizing our meals (to get a good deal), buying the extended warranty and not keeping the paperwork, in a nutshell buying things that we don't need.

You need to determine: is it a *want* or a *need*. If you spend it, WRITE it.

I once heard on the radio: "What does the average American spend $100 on each year that they never use?" The answer was: Clothes that they'll never wear. While this may not be true for everyone, I am sure there are things we can all think of that we buy and never use.

I recently evicted one of my tenants and they did not vacate the property in the time required by the court. This required the Sheriff's department to lock the tenant out. Per Wisconsin statute, if they do not claim their property within 30 days, we are able to sell off their belongings. These tenants did not have the financial discipline to pay their rent on time, but

**Have a Super Fantastic Life.** Have a Super Fantastic Life.

> *The way to get started is to quit talking and begin doing.*
>
> — Walt Disney

they had over 200 recent DVDs that they paid full price for. This would be a cost of over $4000, and could have paid their rent for one year. I know you may be thinking that everyone deserves to have fun and relax. So when my wife and I buy DVDs, we buy them on sale from the movie rental store, two for $7.99 or five for $20.00. At the library you can check them out at no cost to you.

Take a moment by yourself or with your spouse and write down the five most recent items you purchased that you really didn't need. It may be dessert at the end of dinner when you were already stuffed, or the shirt that you bought on sale 16 months ago and still have not worn.

Developing good spending habits is what will lead you on the path to your financial freedom.

A relative of mine recently said she didn't want to give up smoking because this was the only pleasure she had in life right now. I recently read a book by Tony Robbins called *Awaken the Giant Within*. This is by far the best book I have read in my lifetime. A chapter in the book talks about how all choices are made with the preface: "Is this Pain or Pleasure?" When I decided to join Weight Watchers, it was painful, however now it is pleasure as I look forward to going to the meetings and am disappointed if I cannot make them. Just like exercising many years ago, it was Pain at first, but now it is Pleasure, as I look forward to keeping in shape every day. In fact, I have been exercising for so many years that if I miss a day, that causes me pain.

Everyone can look at pain and pleasure in a different way. In Tony's book, it says that Carly Simon failed to perform live for many years because of her stage fright. While Bruce Springsteen felt the same stage fright, he looked at this as pleasure, because he was excited about the joy he would provide to the audience when he performed. They both experienced stage fright but perceived it differently.

*Resolve not to be poor. Whatever you have, spend less.*

— unknown

Changing your spending habits will undoubtedly cause some pain at first, however this will lead you to the path of financial freedom and the pleasure that comes with it.

PMI: Private Mortgage Insurance. Banks require PMI if you have less than a 20% down payment on a home purchase. The rate varies dependent on the amount you have down and your credit score. For example: A $100,000 loan with 95% borrowed and a PMI rate of .89%. This is $890 per year for the life of the loan. The more down on the loan and the better your credit score the lower the PMI will be. The less down and the lower your credit score, the higher your PMI will be. This will cost you several dollars per month for several years. The smart thing to do is pay extra on your loan to get to 20% equity. If homes are appreciating in your area, have your home re-appraised in two to three years. You may have enough equity in your home to have the PMI removed. In this case you should keep your payments the same and have the PMI payment amount go to reducing the principle.

If you have a home loan, a great way to pay it off sooner is to make a payment every two weeks. Most of you have a job that pays every two weeks. If your house payment including PITI (Principle, Interest, Taxes, and Insurance) is $1000 per month, pay the bank $500 every two weeks. A 30-year loan should be paid off in about 22 years and a 15-year loan in about 11 years. On a 30-year loan this will save you $96,000, not counting the interest you would get by investing this amount. Caution: Make sure your bank is applying the payment correctly to reduce your principle.

**Have a Super Fantastic Life.** Have a Super Fantastic Life.

*Everyone in business has heard the old saying: 80% of our sales are produced by 20% of our people. Unfortunately, few seem to know what the 20% are doing that the 80% aren't. Well, let me tell you. The 20% are using a system, and the 80% aren't.*

*unknown*

# 5 Learn What You Do Now Affects You Tomorrow

### Credit Report - Criminal Report - C.L.U.E. Report

**Credit Report**

In 1996 the Packers had the dream season of being 13-3 and going to the Super Bowl. They ended up winning the Super Bowl over the New England Patriots. I was fortunate enough to go to 11 out of the 19 games including all of the playoffs and the Super Bowl. I traveled to Chicago, Seattle, Minnesota, Green Bay, and New Orleans. At every stadium there were several opportunities to receive free Packers stuff by signing up for credit cards. I must have signed up for over a dozen credit cards that season. I would receive the credit card and then cut it up. Years later I went to a wealth building seminar with my wife and one of our assignments after the first day was to find out our credit score. My wife's credit score was over 740. I was shocked, however, to find out my credit score was 640. I thought it would be almost perfect. My credit report showed all those credit cards that I never used. While there was no charge on any of the cards, each card had an impact on my credit score. When you apply for a credit card, it affects your score by 15 points. I eliminated all the credit cards that I no longer used and only kept 4 main ones (VISA, Sears, Menards, Capitol One) that I used mostly for business.

**Have a Super Fantastic Life.** Have a Super Fantastic Life.

Don't be misled into believing that somehow the world owes you a living. The boy who believes that his parents, or the government, or anyone else owes him a livelihood and that he can collect it without labor will wake up one day and find himself working for another boy who did not have that belief and, therefore, earned the right to have others work for him.

*unknown*

I also discovered there was a 45 point reduction on my credit score that showed I was late with one payment on a loan. To my knowledge, I had never missed a payment or been late with a payment throughout my career. The bank that I worked with always took automatic payments out of my checking account. About two years prior to checking my credit, I received a letter from the bank stating I missed a payment. I immediately called and reminded them about the automatic payment from my checking account. They pulled my file and saw that the paperwork was signed but not implemented in the system. They corrected the loan payment to become automatic withdrawal. However, their automated system for tracking late payments had already sent a notice to the credit bureau. The bank didn't think about this, and I didn't even know this type of automatic reporting existed.

You can imagine my dismay at finding my credit score so low. By canceling the numerous, unused credit cards, and by getting my bank to write a letter to the credit bureau explaining their mistake, I was able to get my credit score to over 760 in less than two months.

The moral of this story is that the mistakes/decisions you make can have a negative impact on you and your life without you even being aware. The Packers stuff that I was so eager to get? I no longer have them, as they were disposed of or taken to Goodwill. People have too much stuff that they feel they "need," but in reality it is just a "want."

There are three areas in your life that in today's society will follow you and affect your future: credit/ finances, criminal record, and insurance claim history.

As you can see from my story, your credit report can be repaired or improved over time. Your credit report affects everything financial in your life, like getting a loan for your home or car, or qualifying for credit cards. It will also affect the interest rate you pay (the better your credit score,

**Have a Super Fantastic Life.**

> *Enthusiasm is the gasoline that drives the human body to a destination.*
>
> unknown

the lower your interest rate), the term of your loan, and whether or not you will even qualify for a loan. For example: a $100,000 loan with 6% interest over 30 years has a payment of $599.55 per month. A $100,000.00 loan at 7% over 30 years has a payment of $665.30 per month. The loan at 7% is $65.75 more per month, and over the course of 30 years will cost an additional $23,670. If you took that $65.75 per month and invested it in a savings account at 3% for 30 years it would be $38,314.95. If you invested it in the stock market and had an average rate of return of 10% over 30 years, it would be $148,627.08.

As explained earlier, your credit score will make a difference in the interest rate that you can get for a loan. It will also be used when applying for a rental property. Your score will determine if you qualify for the rental and the size of the security deposit that will be required. The report may also have an affect on any jobs you apply for.

A Good credit score starts at 680. To get a loan with 20% down, you will need a score of 620 or higher. An Elite score is 740, and 850 is a Perfect score.

There are 5 parts of a FICO (Fair Isaac Corporation) score:

35% of the Score is payment history
30% of the Score is how much you owe
15% of the Score is length of credit history
10% of the Score is new credit
10% of the Score is a mix of other factors

Credit scores are very important because they help lenders predict how likely you are to make your payments on time.

Your score will determine if you can get a loan or not. It will also determine the amount of interest you will pay on the loan you are applying for. The higher your score, the higher the likelihood for your loan to be approved and for you to get a lower interest rate.

**Have a Super Fantastic Life.** Have a Super Fantastic Life.

*It is usually not talent that separates people at the top. There is no shortage of talented failures. The key is perseverance and tenacity. Develop the mindset of a top producer.*

unknown

You need to check your credit report on a yearly basis to review for inaccurate or outdated information. To improve your credit score you need to:

1. Go to www.annualcreditreport.com or call (887) 322-8228.
2. Get a copy of your credit report.
3. Look for items that have been paid off or are incorrect.
4. Cancel all credit cards that you DO NOT NEED.
5. Send a letter to the credit agencies explaining discrepancies in your credit report. It is my understanding that they are required to send a letter to the company that reported the negative impact you are questioning. That company has 30 days to respond or it will be removed from your credit report.

The three major companies you can contact for credit reports are:

**TransUnion**
P.O. Box 390
Springfield, PA 10964--0590
www.tuc.com
or www.transunion.com
(800) 888-4213

**Equifax**
P.O. Box 740241
Atlanta, GA 30374-0241
www.equifax.com
(866) 685-1111

**Experian**
P.O. Box 949
Allen, TX 75013
www.experian.com
(800) 200-6020

**Have a Super Fantastic Life.** Have a Super Fantastic Life.

*If you expect the best, you will be the best. Learn to use one of the most powerful laws in the world: change your mental habits to belief instead of doubt. Learn to expect, not to doubt. In doing so, you bring everything into the realm of possibility.*

— Gary Owens

## Sample Letter

To Whom It May Concern at Experian:

I am writing this letter regarding some incorrect reports that your agency is showing on my credit report. The following are incorrect, paid off or no longer open with me.

1. ABC credit card—closed no longer active
2. Xyz credit card—closed no longer active
3. Late payment to BBB has been paid off.
4. Delinquent loan for car. Car has been sold and paid off.

Please correct the above. Please call or email me with any questions at [insert contact info]

It is my understanding that you have 30 days to verify the above or this MUST be removed from my credit history.

Thank you for your prompt attention in getting this corrected.

Sincerely,

New higher credit score guy

---

Make sure you send this letter by certified mail.

Improving your score will get you lower interest rates on home loans, car loans, and credit cards. It will also speed up your loan approvals and get you better offers from more lenders.

### So why is a credit score so important?

The higher your score, the lower interest rate you will pay. A lower score will result in higher interest or inability to get the loan you want at all.

**Have a Super Fantastic Life.** Have a Super Fantastic Life.

> First we will be best, then we will be first.
> — unknown

Credit cards suck you in by telling you that you can save 10% if you open a credit card account at the time of purchase. Almost all credit card companies will offer you something to open a credit card with them (i.e. a discount when you are at a store making a purchase, or 25,000 miles when you get an airplane credit card, and on and on and on). I was told by my bank that every credit card you have will have an impact on your credit score with a 15-point deduction.

Today's society makes it very easy to buy now and pay later. That is what has caused the majority of Americans to be in financial trouble. CHANGE YOUR HABITS TODAY and you will live a much better life tomorrow. Again, it may be painful to begin with, but will bring great financial pleasure in your future.

**Criminal History Report**

The criminal report is now easily accessible and will also follow you throughout your life. Information on everything from a speeding ticket, to misdemeanors and felonies is available. A negative criminal report will certainly have an impact on a job application, being approved for a rental property, and the ability to obtain a loan. Your criminal history will also determine if you qualify to date my daughters. I am in the process of writing another book on how to qualify to date my daughters if you are interested. It will come out when they turn 30 and you will need a $1,000,000 deposit. 30 is the magic number: that is when my daughters are allowed to start dating. ☺

While I am having some fun about dating my daughters, the fact is the mistakes one makes today will continue to affect you for the rest of your life. Buying or dealing drugs, disorderly conduct, or even the night out with the boys where you had a little too much to drink and decided to paint an obscene message on your ex-girlfriend's house will not look good on your job application, rental application, or others.

> *You don't fail overnight. Instead, failure is a few errors in judgment, repeated everyday.*
>
> — Jim Rohn

I will not even consider renting to sexual offenders. This can really affect your life in a negative way. Teach your kids, every mistake you make can follow you for the rest of your life. Even the posts you make on Facebook can come back to haunt you later in life.

A young man and his girlfriend once tried to rent a vacant home of mine. They filled out the rental application, and put nothing under criminal history. I called him to explain the house they wanted to rent was in the entrance to a senior manufactured home park. I told them that the renters in the park are, on average, 70 years old or older and are very concerned about the quiet enjoyment of their homes. Partying, loud music, etc. would create a problem. He said they were very quiet and do not drink.

When we ran the credit and criminal reports we found that they both had underage drinking charges and he had a disorderly conduct charge from about a year prior. We refused to rent to him based on this. He and his mother were very upset with me, arguing that he was under 18 when this happened and it should not have been on his record. I told them I don't make the rules, we run a credit and criminal check on applicants. I explained to them that they lied on the application and they would not get the application fee back. It is stated in writing that any false information on the application would result in being denied tenancy and forfeiting the application fee.

### C.L.U.E. Report

A C.L.U.E. report is a Comprehensive Loss Underwriting Evaluation which determines the frequency of insurance claims. This will affect you as it will determine qualification and rates for insurance. It may also affect qualifying for a loan, approval for a rental property, or getting a job. There have been several times in my career that I have had the potential for an insurance claim, but because the damage was less than $2000 I chose to pay it out of pocket rather

**Have a Super Fantastic Life.** Have a Super Fantastic Life.

*Attitude is a little thing that makes a BIG difference.*

*unknown*

than submit a claim. With the financial crisis our country is in, banks and the federal government are making some of these checks mandatory. Some banks and other lending institutions are making policies that check all these areas of an applicant. They do this to get the best information when approving or denying a loan. Regarding the C.L.U.E. report, if you have had several insurance claims it may throw up a red flag to a lender (can cause higher insurance rates or to be denied insurance altogether).

All of these reports (credit, criminal, C.L.U.E.) will follow you for the rest of your life and are easily accessible to anyone who has your name, social security number, and driver's license number.

How long does information stay on your credit report, C.L.U.E. report, and criminal record?

A friend of mine is the sheriff in the county I live in. I called him about this and he informed me that convictions will stay on your criminal record for your entire life.

C.L.U.E. history is monitored by insurance companies for five or more years.

Late payments, foreclosures, and Chapter 13 bankruptcies stay on your credit report for seven years. Chapter 7 bankruptcies stay on the report for 10 years.

I can't say this enough. THE MISTAKES YOU MAKE TODAY CAN HAUNT YOU THE REST OF YOUR LIFE.

**Have a Super Fantastic Life.** Have a Super Fantastic Life.

*Dare to succeed: Pioneers blaze their path where highways never run.*

*unknown*

# 6
## Do You Really Need That Stuff?
### Credit Cards/ Debit Cards — Buy Now/ Pay Later

How did you get into this mess? We were all born naked. Everyone started with a clean slate. Getting into this mess is caused by BAD habits. You and you alone (or with your spouse) can change your BAD financial habits to GOOD ones. You may have gotten these bad habits from your parents. It may be from your friends. It doesn't really matter where you got them. What matters is recognizing you have them and changing them. If you do not change them you will have a life of financial misery, when you should be living life to the fullest.

Check your credit card interest rates and try to get a lower rate. If you do not pay off your credit card in full (which most of you don't) you MUST stop using this card and get it paid off as soon as possible. Finish reading this paragraph and take action NOW. Put down the book and call your credit card company. Ask them to lower your rate. Tell them you are changing your life and you want to get your credit card and other bills paid off. If they cannot help, tell them "My plan is to get your company paid in full, I need your help by lowering my rate and waiving the monthly charge for not being paid in full. If you cannot help me I am considering meeting with a bankruptcy attorney to go over my options. Can you help me or should I talk

*Statements tend to push people away from you. Questions always pull people towards you.*

*— RJO*

to your supervisor or call _____ the attorney I am considering for bankruptcy." Don't bluff on this, find a local bankruptcy attorney and give them his or her name. Too many times over the course of my career renters have said "my attorney," but when I ask for their attorney's name you would think it was a matter of national security. It's probably because their "attorney" is just the person sitting next to them at the bar. Giving the credit card company an attorney's name will let them know you are serious.

You can use this same method with all of your debts. Just be prepared to follow through.

We have become a society of fulfilling our wants before our needs. What is a need? Maslow says our basic needs are food, shelter, and clothing.

Every teenager thinks a cell phone/Blackberry/iPhone is a need. While not opposing a cell phone, I will be one of the first people having my cell phone implanted under my skin. My generation all grew up without cell phones. Are they time savers? You bet. But we can live without them. All you really need to survive is food and shelter.

There are so many things that we perceive we need, when they are really just wants or desires. As stated above all you really need is food and shelter. To get ahead or get out of debt you may need to eliminate some of the things that you feel are needs but are in reality a want. For example: Cable TV, premium channels, the internet, cell phone, extra car, and on and on.

Society and marketing make it so easy to fulfill your wants. I can remember as a kid, we had three channels of TV with no remote control. When a Captain Crunch commercial would come on, I would immediately want to go get the Captain Crunch out of the cupboard and eat a bowl. This may sound foolish, but that made me feel special, that I was eating the cereal that was being advertised on TV.

> There is nothing that will damage your attitude more quickly than the negative comments of others. You must listen to yourself and achieve!
>
> — unknown

Society has made it so easy to buy now and pay later. Buy furniture, appliances, and electronics today and there are no payments or interest until next year. This is routine and getting approval for this is very easy. Then what happens is when you forget that you owe this amount and the payment becomes due, you need to pick up the pace on the treadmill of life. The ads for these items make you WANT them and make you feel like they are a NEED, when in fact they are just a want and something you can do without. You buy these wants and your financial treadmill keeps going faster and faster while you try to catch up on the payments owed.

Sometimes when I pick up my children they will say "Dad I am *starving*." I will remind them that they don't know what starving is; neither they nor I have ever truly experienced "starving." Most of us have made this comment: it makes us feel the need to satisfy our hunger. Routinely these comments from my kids will cause me to take them through the fast food line, believing their desire for food is a need when really it is a want. The cost of satisfying their want can add up to a significant amount over the course of a week, month, year, or a lifetime. Not to mention the side effects of fast food on their health. We all know fast food is not always the best choice for us. When picking up your children from school or other events, be prepared: have snacks that they can choose from and that will save you and your family money. I have worked on hundreds of large projects, costing many thousands of dollars and in some cases millions of dollars. When budgeting for projects, it is not the big items that exceed the budget. Usually, it is the small ones that keep adding up. Be prepared for when you pick up your kids, bring a healthy snack that costs considerably less than going through the drive thru. While it may be a minimal amount each time, the drive thru may be three miles out of your way (six miles total) and this adds to the total cost. Gas prices keep going up. Two kids' meals ($3.50

**Have a Super Fantastic Life.** Have a Super Fantastic Life.

*Wishing will not bring success, but planning, persistence, and a burning desire will.*

*unknown*

each) are $7.00, plus $2.00 for gas, equals $9.00 each trip. If you do this once a week it will cost $468.00 per year.

Trust me on the buy now, pay later plan. For example: An ad for living room furniture, on sale now for $1500 and no payments for one year. I will guarantee that you can save at least 10% if you pay cash. Paying cash will save you money on all big purchases. Not only can it eliminate interest on a loan, you could save money on the total cost. When you see the ads that say "Buy now and no payments for one year," talk to the right person and you can save at least 10% by paying in full with cash today.

If you save up and pay cash for the large screen TV (which is really a want, not a need) you will save money and not have the monthly payments for something that is obsolete by the time you have paid it off.

I have worked with numerous people that are still making payments on cars that don't run, stereo systems that don't work, or things they don't use. Buying now and paying later is a disease that many individuals have contracted. The good news is that this disease is curable, but the cure can be challenging to say the least. You have to change your spending habits to ones that make better financial sense for your future.

Remember: when you have a higher priced item that you feel is a need (or a can't-do-without), you should have a conversation with yourself (or your parents, spouse, or good friends) to determine if this is really a need.

I am not suggesting that you live each day riding a used bike to work and eating peanut butter sandwiches (although there may be a time to do this, also). I am suggesting that you save for your wants and make good, sound financial decisions. Changing your spending habits will allow you in later years to fulfill your wants and pay cash for them. Believe me: if you get into the correct spending habits early in life, you will have less wants and a more enjoyable future.

**Have a Super Fantastic Life.** Have a Super Fantastic Life.

*If you think education is expensive, try ignorance.*

— Derek Bok

# DO YOU NEED THAT?

The first time my wife and I went to Mexico, we were lying on the beach when one of the many vendors came by selling carved wood items. One of them was an eagle, and I was very interested in buying it. I must have negotiated with 20 different vendors over the course of the next five days of our trip. Celeste kept telling me, "You don't need that, what are you going to do with that?" I had made up my mind that I would pay a maximum of $100 for it. I am so happy none of them came down to $100, the lowest was $120. The good news is I did not buy it. If I would have, it would be packed away or given to Goodwill by now.

## Do you really need that?

Several years ago I went to a convention and the trade show was huge. I bought six items that I thought would make my business better and save me time. What I found out was I only implemented two of the six I bought.

What I learned from that (or should I say a rule I made for myself for the future) was not to buy anything until the last day of the convention. By doing this I got the four to six things that I felt I *had to have* down to one or none.

**Mike's Wait a Day Rule:** Wait at least ONE DAY before buying. Marketing and advertising is designed to make you WANT and feel that you MUST have this or that item NOW. It is amazing how the desire is gone for most things after waiting a day. Just this last week I heard on the radio that a guy had a like-new men's bike for sale. He paid over $400 and was selling for $150. It sounded like a good deal and I thought I could probably get it for $100. I called and talked to him but could not make it that day to see the bike. The next day I started asking myself, "Will I really use it and what is wrong with the bike I have?" The next day I threw his number away. If I could have seen the bike within one to two hours of hearing the ad, I would have bought something I did not need. Make a rule for yourself. WAIT at least ONE DAY before buying.

**Have a Super Fantastic Life.** Have a Super Fantastic Life.

*Comfort overtakes us all when we're least prepared for it. Comfort makes cowards of us all.*

*— unknown*

## DO YOU NEED THAT?

Too many people try to keep up with the Joneses. Who are the Joneses? They may be your neighbors, friends, or relatives. They have IT, why shouldn't I have IT? The problem is that we buy things because other people have those things and then we have to run faster and faster on the treadmill of our financial payments. This adds more and more stress to our lives, and we become more frustrated by these purchases than happy.

Advertisers get it. They say "Call in the next 10 minutes and get two for the price of one." Baloney! You can order it a month later and still get the two for one deal. They are trying to get you to act NOW. They know if you don't buy now the odds of you buying later go WAY down. See my rule above and wait at least a day.

You might say, "Mike, I am only going to be here today!" In that case, come back to that store or vendor at the end of the day. You might still have to have it, but my guess is you will have changed your mind.

"Buy now for three monthly payments of $29.99, plus shipping and handling." That will work out to over $110 for something you can live without. The advertisers make it look like you MUST have it and that it is cheap and easy. Now is the only time to buy or you will not get this special deal!!!

Look at the credit card commercials. There are several out there that imply paying with CASH makes you look abnormal or like you are inconveniencing everyone else by paying in cash. They are trying to get you in the HABIT of buying things with your credit cards.

In my opinion credit cards are the worst thing our country has ever come up with. Do I use them? Yes, but thank God I always pay them off in full and on time. Most people, (over 51%) do not pay off the balance on their card in full and do not pay it off on time, causing more expense. The biggest problem is that they buy more than they need.

**Have a Super Fantastic Life.**

*Find a way today to make changes in yourself instead of someone else. Sometimes the results are the same.*

*unknown*

Impulse buying: I've had a rough day and I am going to reward myself. Go out for dinner, stop for a few drinks, go to the movies, buy the $4 cup of coffee, and on and on. We all do this and then feel bad after we have spent the money. **Spending your way to happiness is not the solution.** 96% of Americans will never achieve being debt free.

Timeshare salespeople. I don't know about you but I hate going to the dentist. However, I would prefer a root canal over sitting through another timeshare presentation. They make you feel like the scum of the earth unless you buy. They promise you everything, and do not let you leave unless you buy.

The first time I was dumb enough to sit through one, I told them I was not going to buy, but being in real estate I wanted to know the price. They then asked if my girlfriend and I were married, and we were not. They said we did not qualify, took us into another room, and told us we would not get the promised promotion. To say I was upset was an understatement. I asked to talk to a supervisor and finally they got the head person on the phone. They continued to ask me to leave. I said one of two things is going to happen, I told them it was their choice. Either I was getting my two tickets to the Hawaiian Luau or the police would be called. They gave me my two tickets. Trust me DO NOT go to a timeshare presentation. EVER.

The definition of Consumer: An individual who buys products or services for personal use. This is someone who can be influenced by marketing and advertisements. Influence is the key: marketing wants to influence what you buy and when.

The best time to save money is before you spend it. Have a list when you go shopping and stick to that list. Search the internet for coupons for the items you are going to buy before you go shopping. The average family of four can save over $200 per month by buying items on sale and using

**Have a Super Fantastic Life.** Have a Super Fantastic Life.

> The young man knows the rules, but the old man knows the exceptions.
>
> — Oliver Wendell Holmes

coupons. Prybuy.com, DealChicken.com, and similar sites are a great way to get coupons and deals before you buy.

Ways to save money:
    Eat at home.
    Do your own laundry.
    Clean your own car.
    Cut back on or get rid of cable TV.
    Phone service: Are you using your home line or can you do without it?
    Extended warranties: If it is going to break, it will usually do so in the first couple months. DON'T buy them.
    Cancel your gym membership. Buy used equipment, walk or run outside, or use things around your home.

*If at first you do not succeed, try another way.*

   *unknown*

# 7 Credit is Not Your Friend

Who are you working for? Yourself, or the people you owe money to? The borrower is slave to the lender (Proverbs 22:7).

My wife and I went on a cruise and had a "super fantastic" time. Afterwards, I had a question about my bill, as the cruise lines make it very easy for you to spend money. You get a Sail and Sign™ card when you board the ship. This is like a credit card and all of your charges get put on it. It is the only way you can buy things on the ship. When waiting in line to get my question answered, there was a young man who was discussing his bill with the clerk because he had over $1200 in charges. It sounded like the majority was for alcohol. He was furious with the clerk regarding all of the charges on his card. And at one point he proclaimed, "How am I supposed to pay for this when I had to borrow money to take this trip?" He complained that the girls he was buying drinks for didn't want to give him their phone numbers. I had to actually bite my lip to keep from laughing. The cards for my wife and I had a combined total of $250, which included some photos and other souvenirs. This young man still had his trip to pay for plus over $1000 more than we had left to pay because we had the trip paid for in advance. We had saved and paid before we took the trip.

**Have a Super Fantastic Life.** Have a Super Fantastic Life.

> You've got to be very careful if you don't know where you're going, because you might not get there.
>
> — Yogi Berra

In addition, the young man complained that he shouldn't have been able to spend $1200 because his credit card limit was $1000, and how could they let him exceed that limit? The cruise ship didn't care, they just wanted him to spend more money. I don't know what happened with his credit card when he got home or how he settled his bill before he got off the ship (as is required), but I do know that he shouldn't have gone on a trip that he couldn't pay for.

Most places, if not all, make it very easy for you to spend money. Taking a vacation (like a cruise) is something that my wife and I thoroughly enjoy. We have budgeted for a vacation every year that we have been married. We originally would rotate our vacations one year with kids, one year without. However, we quickly decided that we enjoyed our vacations too much and we started taking two vacations each year, one with just us and one with our kids. These vacations used to be a week long, but now after 14 years of marriage and careful planning, we schedule a 10-day vacation for us and a second two-week vacation with the kids.

Whether you like to vacation, buy jewelry, own technology, or whatever: **you need to discipline yourself to save now and buy later.** Marketing is geared to spend now and pay later, to spend your money even before you make it. Banks will offer home equity lines of credit that suggest you borrow to take your winter vacation where it is warm and sunny and pay later. Easy credit since 2007 has become somewhat more difficult, but it is still readily available.

I have made the mistake in the past of going out for drinks and setting up a bar tab. This quite frankly is STUPID.

At Christmas, we have a large group of friends that get together at a local establishment for Christmas cheer. One year, I set up a bar tab when we arrived and the more I drank, the more I bought for others. Not only that, several of the people at the party took advantage of me and put their drinks on my bar tab without my authorization. By

*Each of us is, ultimately, part of the solution or part of the problem.*

*unknown*

the time I left, my bar tab was $190.00. This may not seem like a lot of money in New York City, but drinks in Wisconsin at the time cost under $2.00 for beer or mixers.

In a situation like this, it makes much more sense to bring what you want to spend and leave your credit cards and other money at home. This will make it difficult, if not impossible, to overspend.

GREAT spending habits are the keys to financial freedom. My wife and I plan to travel extensively when we retire in our mid-fifties. We have put together a financial plan that will allow us to fulfill our dreams.

Today's marketing, including TV, radio, billboard, and certainly internet, is geared to make their products a must-have. But as stated earlier, there is a huge difference from a need and want. Remember you only need food, shelter, and clothing, and this can be done very reasonably.

I am not suggesting you don't enjoy some of the finer things in life, but to put yourself in a financial position to enjoy more of them. As I am writing this book in my home, I look around at all the things that I have accumulated. I thought some of the artwork was an investment when I bought it. Now, as I look around, I am confident that I couldn't get more for it than I paid.

Debit cards are good in the sense that you can't spend what you don't have. However, they make spending very easy. A friend of mine told me about her daughter who is in college, and happened to notice three withdrawals for a local tavern. This type of withdrawal is all too easy to make especially after you have had a few drinks. If you can't control your spending, take only the cash with you that you want to spend, and leave all other credit and debit cards at home. That is why a lot of taverns and other similar places have ATM machines. They make it very easy for you to access money so you can spend more.

**Have a Super Fantastic Life.**

*Money talks but credit has an echo.*

*Bob Thaves*

If you are using your debit card, you must know what fee the ATM company is charging you. Some companies take $1-5 for each transaction.

I have never used an ATM card, and I sure can't get my arms around having to pay to get my money. Find out how you can avoid this fee (i.e. using your own bank). ATM companies are getting rich off these small incremental transactions. While no one is going to go broke over two dollars, it is the accumulation of this amount over time. It is just a plain bad habit to pay to get your money out of an ATM.

If you take out $20 and have a $2 fee, you are paying the ATM company 10%. That is 10% for one day of interest. No wonder these companies are making money.

## Borrowing Money

There are times when borrowing money makes sense. I have purchased numerous rental properties in the course of my life. I have borrowed the full amount and paid interest on these loans until the property has been paid off in full or sold. Owning rental properties can give you the passive income and the cash flow that makes borrowing money make sense. An example is buying a duplex where the principle, interest, taxes, and insurance payment equals $1000 per month and the rental income for both sides is $1500 per month. You would have a positive cash flow of $500 per month.

Owning your own home is highly recommended because you "need" shelter. I would recommend owning a home and living within your means. For example: if you need a two bedroom home, and you find one that is sufficient to meet your needs to rent for $500 per month, I recommend you look to buy a home that would keep your payments at a maximum of $500 per month instead of renting. Keep in mind you will need to have money to pay for the maintenance and repairs, so you should start saving for this in advance.

*It doesn't cost anything to be nice.*

*unknown*

You should have an emergency fund of at least $1000 and increase this by $50 per month until you have at least $5000. This will vary depending on where you live and the cost of living. The emergency fund should end up being equal to six months of all your living expenses. It will take time to build up your emergency fund (approximately four years) and the way to do it is by calculating your monthly expenses times 6 and dividing it by 48. For example: if your monthly expenses are $2000 x 6 = $12,000. Divided by 48 = $250. You need to set aside $250 per month until you reach $12,000. By the time you have this money set aside your monthly expenses may have gone up and you may need to readjust this. You also may have had to draw from the emergency fund and may have to extend your payments until this is replenished. The definition of emergency for this fund is not that your favorite musician is in town and you need $200 for front row seats. This fund is to be used for unanticipated situations such as a major car repair, loss of income due to illness or job loss, unexpected home repairs like a new furnace, or the death of a loved one that requires travel expenses to go to the funeral.

When you own your home, you may qualify for a home equity line of credit. This can be beneficial if you are looking to use this money for investment purposes. Do NOT, and I repeat DO NOT ever use a home equity loan to pay off your debt on your credit card and other non-secured debt. While it may seem good because you can pay off other unsecured debt with the home equity loan's lower interest rate, and the interest on the home equity loan is tax deductible, the problem is in three years or more, most people have acquired the same amount of credit card debt again. Now they owe more money on their home (which would have had some equity) and they then are right back to having $25,000 charged on their credit cards. The treadmill keeps going and going and going....

**Have a Super Fantastic Life.** Have a Super Fantastic Life.

*Success is a journey as well as a destination!*

*unknown*

# 8 Budget

The six-letter word that everyone hates: Budget.

Most people think that when it comes to budgeting their money, "What is the use? I never have enough money anyway." Just like when trying to lose weight, if you don't have a plan you will never lose weight. For many of you reading this book, there is too much *month* left at the end of the *money*.

Setting up a budget is the first step. Sticking to it is the hard part but can be the key to financial independence.

What is amazing to me is how it is not the big things that mess up your budget, but the little things that add up: the can of soda, the trip through the drive thru, pack of cigarettes, renting a movie. If you have a house payment or rent of $500 per month, you know where your money went. If you are using your credit card to pay for things routinely and paying the minimum payment, you are paying very little of the principle. I am not suggesting you can't have a life by not being able to get that cup of coffee or go out with friends, but you should plan for that.

For example: If you are working at a fast food company and your net pay is $7.00 per hour, you make $14,560 per year, or $1213.33 take home (minus taxes/insurance/social

*What are the chances?*

*Mike Zurfluh*

security) per month. If this is your income, it would benefit you to have a roommate. If you are married, hopefully your spouse is working and you have two incomes, as it is nearly impossible to live on $1213.33 per month take home pay.

I know in some places it may be difficult to find a rental for $600 per month for a two-bedroom home. However, in my area you can get a pretty nice rental for this amount of money. The following example will use $600 per month for a rental unit.

The first thing you should do when you start budgeting is to pay yourself first.

Take a minimum of 10% of what you earn and set it aside in savings. In this example that is $242.67 per month based on two people working, with take home pay of $2426.66.

Expenses per month for two working people:

| | |
|---|---|
| Savings (Pay Yourself First) | $243 |
| Rent | $600 |
| Clothing/incidentals | $100 |
| Food | $300 |
| Utilities (gas/sewer/water/electric) | $150 |
| Cable/Phone/Internet | $100 |
| Cell phone | $100 |
| Entertainment | $50 |
| Dining Out | $50 |
| Car Payment | $200 |
| Car Insurance | $100 |
| Emergency fund | $100 |
| Car/Gas/oil | $250 |
| Total | $2343 |

Leaving $83 per month. This does not include health insurance or anything else not stated above.

Where can you trim your budget? The one area that should never be touched is your savings. Unless you use your savings for a down payment on a house in the future.

**Have a Super Fantastic Life.** Have a Super Fantastic Life.

> *Be greedy when others are scared and be scared when others are greedy.*
>
> — Warren Buffett

If you have good credit, you can purchase an $80,000 home and keep your payment, including taxes and insurance close to $600 per month. I know there are areas where you cannot purchase a home for $80,000 and you may need to think about relocating to a different area.

Keep in mind the amount set aside for housing is about 25% of your income. In bigger cities, where you can't find housing prices like this, the typical pay at a fast food restaurant brings you home more than $7.50 per hr.

The example above is for low-income individuals. Below is the breakdown for class types, U.S. income levels, and population percentage.

Approximate Social Class Percentage in 2005:

Lower Class ($8K and below) 14-20%
Working Class ($15K - $30K) about 32%
Lower Middle Class ($35K - $75K) about 32%
Upper Middle Class ($75K - $100K) about 15%
Upper Class (more than $200K) about 1.5%

Credit: WikiAnswers 2013

Like I said: losing weight is not easy, and neither is reaching financial independence. You should be able to cut from your food budget: shopping at discount food stores, clipping coupons, and buying things that are on sale. You can also make sure your prescription medications are generic, and non-prescriptions can be store brand.

You can cut your clothing budget down to $10 or $20 per month by shopping at thrift stores, Goodwill, or rummage sales. You can work on cutting your utilities by turning off lights, turning heat down at night or when you are not at home, and doing laundry with a full load. Use air conditioning sparingly and remember to turn off or up when not home. You can also eliminate cable, internet, and phone. This may seem unrealistic for many, but not having these items will give you an opportunity to save more money. Al-

*They still keep score in dollars.*

— unknown

ready the new generation does not have "home" phones or landlines. In 20 years, kids may not know what a home telephone looked like.

Which reminds me of a story about my daughter, Macie. She was about seven years old and we stopped at an estate sale. She found an old, black rotary phone and she had no clue what it was for. She ended up buying it for $1.00 and we still have it in our kitchen today. Kids today have no knowledge about the "party lines" like my family had when we grew up. You would pick up the phone and could hear the conversation going on. We had to wait until one of our neighbors finished using the phone to make a call. There were several people on each line.

You can also save money on your automobile. If one or both of you live close to your work, you can walk to work or car pool. Having one car as compared to two will save considerably. For starters, you will only have insurance on one car. You will also save on maintenance and gas as you will not be duplicating driving to certain areas.

My mother used to tell me about how my dad would work eight hours in the paper mill and then walk to Haessly's concrete plant and make cement block for $1.00 per hour. He did this for several years until they had enough cash to pay for a car. They paid $4500 for their first and only house. They borrowed the money from a relative and paid it off in less than five years. I know what you are thinking: "Where can you buy a house for $4500?" For the most part, nowhere. But at that time, my dad was getting more than minimum wage working in the mill and making cement blocks to supplement his income. Today, the mill workers are making around $20 per hour. So a $4500 house back then (1950's) x 20 is a $90,000 house today. It can be done.

You can save on entertainment expenses by doing things such as renting a movie (or getting a movie from the library where there is no cost), playing cards with family or

*The real measure of your wealth is how much you'd be worth if you lost all your money.*

— unknown

friends, playing board games, or picnics in the park (or your own front yard). Or have a fun night with other couples or friends that may involve a game of volleyball, throwing the Frisbee, swimming in the lake or sledding/tubing down a hill. Not only are these things free, it is also better for you to be out in the fresh air. Plus, the exercise is always good for everyone involved.

Friends can take turns watching each other's children. Have a DATE NIGHT. My wife and I do this at least once per month. It may be a dinner out or renting a movie. It may be going to a local play. It is very important for our relationship and can be done VERY inexpensively.

You can also look for ways to create more income, like volunteering to work overtime, or improving your performance to get a raise. If the job you have does not have overtime, you may want to look for a second part-time job. Some companies will even pay for additional education, provided you maintain a certain grade level. You may also want to consider joining the National Guard or military as they have many programs that will get you a college education for free. When I finished my college degree there were two local companies that paid for their employees education. They had to do it on their own time and get a B grade or better. The more knowledgeable you are, the more value you bring to your employer, which should coincide with the income that you receive.

In my company, the employees with a great work ethic, who almost never miss work and are willing to go the extra mile, are the ones that are paid the most and would certainly be the last jobs that I would eliminate if downsizing would have to occur.

Most employees feel they are underpaid for the work that they do. Remember: no one is holding a gun to your head and forcing you to work the job that you have. Doing the job and exceeding the expectations of your employer may not

*A rising tide raises all boats.*

*unknown*

get you ahead with that particular employer, but this will build the habits that will make you successful down the road. There are always opportunities for new jobs. A lot of employers, such as myself, will ask employees and/or business associates if they know someone who will do a particular job before they advertise to hire a new employee.

The bottom line is this: With budgeting, the only way to have more money is to spend less, make more, or a combination of both. This doesn't have to be your budget forever but you should set a goal, accomplish it, and then at a certain point reevaluate to determine your next budget.

The main reason to set a budget is so you are not spending money on "doo dads" and other wasteful items. My wife and I had a goal of paying our house off. When we achieved that goal, we set other goals. When we were first married, we took one vacation a year to a warm place, such as Mexico. We decided how much we loved spending time in Mexico during the cold Wisconsin winters, so we researched and read books on how to buy properties in Mexico. In 2006, we went to Mexico with a plan to find a condo and buy it. We were looking for a minimum of a two-bedroom, two-bath condo but would prefer three bedrooms and two baths. Our budget was $350,000. What we found would meet all of our needs was a three-bedroom, three-bath condo priced at $450,000. We did end up purchasing the condo for $410,000, and by the time we had it furnished and decorated we had $450,000 into it. Through hard work and a dedicated plan, we were able to pay this off in three years.

At the time of writing this book, my wife and I are both 49 years old. Our youngest daughter is in the sixth grade, and if our plans go as scheduled, we will be in a position to spend the majority of our winters on the beach in Mexico within seven years.

One of my wife's dreams is to be able to travel and see the world. This is something we both would enjoy, and with

*The only short cut to success is hard work.*

*unknown*

planning I believe we will be able to do this. Our plan is to be debt free, with all of our investment properties, home and condo paid off by age 58. This will leave us in a financial position to do the things we have dreamed and planned together.

One of the ways we will be able to do this is by renting out our condo. When we are in Mexico in the winter, finding a renter who wants it for a week or more will give us a great travel opportunity with all the advantages available on the internet. Whether it is a cruise, a trip to an exotic island, touring Europe or other parts of the world, they will be adventures that we both will look forward to.

Keep in mind my wife and I have both worked very hard throughout our careers. My wife has a college degree in nursing. While working as a nurse, she went back to school and received her Master's Degree. This allowed her to receive numerous promotions and increases in pay and benefits.

The education I received allowed me to be more successful and make a higher level of income, allowing us to continually have more money to put in our budget. One of the great things is that my wife and I are on the same page when it comes to spending money. We are both what I would classify as very frugal, always looking for the best value. As we have grown together and matured, we have both realized that material things are not as important. While we both continue to have dreams and goals for the future (two of which are building a new home and having a larger condo in Mexico), we will continue to work to achieve these goals without putting our financial position in jeopardy.

> Setting a budget and sticking to it will cement the habits that will make financial independence achievable for everyone.

**Have a Super Fantastic Life.** Have a Super Fantastic Life.

*The best way to predict the future is to create it.*

— unknown

## Emergency fund

After you have found out how much you spend per month, you need to develop an emergency fund. You will want to have the equivalent of six months expenses saved up. For example: if your expenses are $2000 per month, save $12,000 for your emergency fund.

The emergency fund is not to be used for a great deal on vacations. It is to be used for:

> The transmission on the car that needs to be replaced. $2000
>
> The furnace in the house that needs to be replaced. $2500
>
> You lose your job and unemployment is only $1500 per month, so you will need to use $500 per month from your emergency fund.

After you have taken money out of your emergency fund, you need to rebuild it to the six-month supply as soon as you can. This needs to be reviewed every year to make sure you account for any changes and/or inflation.

The monthly expense worksheet helps determine your budget. Fill it out, eliminate the money that is wasteful spending, and then what is left you can use for the basis of your budget.

**Have a Super Fantastic Life.** Have a Super Fantastic Life.

*When you open the flood gates you cannot tell the water where to go.*

*unknown*

# 9 Marriage

I believe that 90% of your happiness or 90% of your misery will be because of who you marry!!!

There is a plaque on the wall in my office that my sister Chris gave me. The saying on top of the plaque says, "Marry the right person, this will account for 90% of your happiness or misery." Of course she gave it to me after I was married (not that that would have made a difference). However, this saying is so true. With over half of the marriages in the U.S. ending in divorce, my belief is the big reason for divorce starts with financial troubles.

When you meet the man or woman of your dreams, you think that you cannot live without them. Then, as you get further along in your relationship or marriage, you realize no one is perfect, including yourself (with the exception of my wife, just ask her). Marriage, like anything else in life (work, sports, playing a musical instrument) gets easier as you work on it. Most people, including myself, find it difficult to discuss the money and spending habits of someone else. Money is so personal.

I am working with an individual that is losing his house to the bank. His wife had ran up several thousand dollars in credit card debt. He lost his job due to an injury. They

The elevator to success is out of order, you will have to use the stairs one step at a time.

*unknown*

had a great house, luxury cars, etc., and it all came crashing down. He is going to lose his house to the bank and get nothing. He will be living disability check to disability check. He made big bucks when he was working, but they lived the BIG LIFE and now will just be getting by.

**BEFORE YOU ARE MARRIED, DISCUSS FINANCES.**

What are your assets? How do you spend money? Who pays the bills? Where does your money go? What are your financial personalities (i.e. tight, frugal, spendthrift, disciplined, undisciplined, etc.)?

The following is a list of questions that you should discuss with your boyfriend/girlfriend before getting married (I would recommend even before getting engaged).

1. Do you want children? If so, how many?
2. Do you both plan on working after you have children?
3. Do you plan on working full time or part time?
4. What income do you make today and expect to make in the future?
5. Do you want to own your own home?
6. Do you use a credit card?
7. Do you have more than one credit card?
8. If you use a credit card, do you pay it in full each month or pay the minimum?
9. What current debts do you have?
10. Are you behind on any payments?
11. What are your current assets?
12. Do you want to take vacations?
13. Do you plan on saving for vacations or going on vacation and then paying it off?
14. Do you want to have your own money?
15. Do you want to have a separate checking account?
16. If we have separate accounts how will we pay the bills?

**Have a Super Fantastic Life.**

*Impossible only describes the degree of difficulty.*

David Phillips

## MARRIAGE

17. Do you plan on having a prenuptial agreement?
18. How long do you believe it should take to pay off our home loan?
19. How much money per month should we save... a specific dollar amount or a percentage of income?
20. Do you gamble? If so, how often?
21. Do you smoke, use alcohol or drugs, if so how often?
22. Do you plan on having a budget?
23. How often, or how much, do you plan on spending per month on entertainment (dinner, movie, lunch, coffee, etc.)
24. How are your parents doing financially?
25. How much should be spent on a wedding?
26. When our children are older, do you believe they should get a job?
27. Do you think we should pay for our kids' cell phones?
28. Do you believe we should buy our children a car?
29. Do you believe we should pay for our children's post high school education?
30. What do you want to do when you retire?
31. What are your spiritual beliefs and practices?

If you can't talk to the person you want to spend the rest of your life with, who can you talk to? DON'T GET MARRIED IF YOU CAN'T DISCUSS MONEY AND THE QUESTIONS ABOVE!!!

I know what you are thinking. I love this person more than anyone in the world. I can't live without them. We have all felt that way at times. That feeling is certainly not the reason that over 50% of all marriages end in divorce.

I've only been married one time. However, my wife was married before. Divorce is NOT an easy situation for anyone involved. Not for the divorcing husband and wife, not

**Have a Super Fantastic Life.**

*Insurance industry statistics let us look ahead 40 years into the future and see what will happen to 100 people who are now age 25. Of these 100, 1 will be wealthy, 4 will be comfortable and have all the money they need to live on and retire on, 5 will still be working in order to live, 36 will have died, 54 will be dependent upon family, friends or some government agency for their retirement livelihood! Why, 5% of these people had clearly defined goals! The other 95% followed any path marked, If you don't know where you are going, any road will take you there!*

*unknown*

for the children involved, and not for the spouse and children who are brought into the new marriage. I could write an entire book on this subject.

The bottom line is that we all change over time. The person you thought you could not live without is not as perfect as you thought they were, and, guess what... you are not as perfect as they thought you were. But a divorce is not a way to attain your financial independence.

Taking the time to go over and answer the questions above can make the difference between a lasting marriage and a divorce.

If you cannot honestly answer the questions above with the person of your dreams then you should not get married. PERIOD.

*Opportunities are never lost. The other person takes those you miss.*

*Wesley Forcier*

# 10 Assets

How long can you live without a job? Do you have enough passive income to not work? Passive income is money you make even when you are not working; i.e. money in the stock market, interest paid on savings, and rental income.

If you earn enough passive income to live the rest of your life without working then you are truly wealthy!

The two sources of my own passive income are from real estate investments and money investments (stocks, bonds, and retirement funds).

As stated earlier, real estate investments (when paid in full) can produce significant passive income. They can pay you money 24 hours a day, 7 days a week, 365 days a year. For example if you have a duplex that is getting rent of $750 per side, $1500 for both units. When this is paid in full after expenses, taxes, insurance, vacancies, and maintenance, you should still have a positive cash flow of over $1000 per month. CHA-CHING!!!

When you have money investments in the form of stocks, bonds, or retirement funds and you can live off the return on these investments without touching the principle, then you are truly wealthy and can live the life you have dreamed.

**Have a Super Fantastic Life.** Have a Super Fantastic Life.

Choose your friends and associates wisely. In Proverbs 13:20 Solomon writes, "He that walks with wise men shall become wise. But a companion of fools shall be destroyed."

*unknown*

My goal in writing this book was to plant the seeds of achieving financial freedom in the readers' mind. Pick one thing to start within the next 30 days. This will give you the foundation to continue to change your life for the better. It can be something small, like cutting up one credit card or eliminating one latte, or something bigger like starting to set a budget. If you are in a total financial disaster, trying to change everything overnight is not going to work. Build a foundation by starting with one step and adding another for a minimum of 30 days. Remember to build in small rewards along the way. I have a wish list for our house. Every time I sell a home that I own, I buy one of the items on my wish list with a small portion of the profits. When I have completed that list, I will make a new wish list of things I want to do or places I want to go with my wife and family. I will keep paying down debt but also rewarding myself and my family along the way. The journey is the reward! Make your journey a great one.

For those of you who are reading this chapter, you have already taken a very big first step. If you are married or have a significant other, have them read this book. You should both list and prioritize the top seven things you want to work at to give you the financial freedom you both deserve.

At the time of writing this book, our country and the world is in the middle of one of the most challenging financial periods since the great depression. Yet I still see the opportunities and hope for the future through you, the reader.

We live in the greatest country in the world and you have the opportunity to make your life be the best it can be.

## Assets

What is an asset? Is your car an asset? Furniture, timeshare, college education? While you can look at these as assets, I believe they are not assets from a wealth-building standpoint. My definition of an asset is something of value that produces a positive return. While having a college ed-

*Attitude: The greatest discovery of any generation is that a human being can alter his life by altering his attitude.*

*William James*

## ASSETS

ucation can help you build wealth, it does not by itself produce a positive return. Furniture, if you are lucky, is worth about 50% of what you paid for it the day it is delivered and goes down from there. Timeshares? Good luck selling it, most people I know give them away.

When money flows in it is an ASSET.

When money goes out it is a LIABILITY.

Examples:

A duplex that you purchase and then rent out. For this example, assume you buy a $100,000 duplex with 10% down, a $10,000 investment of your own money.

If you are getting $600 per side for rent that is a total of $1200 per month income.

Your expenses may be as follows:

| | |
|---|---|
| Principle and Interest (P&I) payments ($90,000 loan at 6% interest over 20 years): | $644.79 per month |
| Taxes: | $150 per month |
| Insurance: | $30 per month |
| Repairs and maintenance: | $50 per month |
| Vacancy: | $50 per month |
| Total: | $924.79 per month |

This leaves a positive cash flow of $275.21 per month.

Over 12 months this is $3302.52, a 33% return on your initial investment of $10,000. I would definitely consider that an ASSET.

Other assets are:

Savings accounts (with interest return).

IRA (tax advantages).

**Have a Super Fantastic Life.** Have a Super Fantastic Life.

> *Restaurants are just part of life. The typical adult now averages 5.8 restaurant occasions in a week.*
>
> — The National Restaurant Association 2008 Restaurant Industry Pocket Factbook

**Retirement plans.** I believe company, state, and federal plans will be disappearing in the future. Most already are replaced with company matching funds (i.e. you put 3% into your 401K and the company will match this). The company usually has a cap, approximately 4%.

**Social Security.** I would not consider this an asset. I do believe Social Security will be there when I retire, but I don't want to count on that for my retirement as I am not positive what age I will have to be to collect and what the amount will be. Yes, Social Security will give you an estimate of what you will get and at what age now, based on how much you have paid in. This, in my opinion, will have to change. The government deficit is at unsustainable levels. Something will have to change and I believe Social Security will also have changes made to it.

You have to remember that Social Security was not designed as a retirement plan. It was designed to help families survive when they lost a loved one or they became disabled and could no longer work.

I recommend you make a list of everything you have that is an asset and a liability.

Make 5 columns when you make your list or go to www.getzurf.com to print out a copy.

> Money Watchers
> I will not spend what
> I do not have

**Asset**: Cash - Savings - Stocks - Bonds - Real Estate

**Liability**: Anything you owe money on.
        Credit cards - car loan - student loan - etc

**Have a Super Fantastic Life.** Have a Super Fantastic Life.

*Each day you make one of two choices for that day of your life, you either feed your confusion or strengthen your clarity. Whichever one you choose, you then implement behaviors to make it happen.*

unknown

## ASSETS

| Date | Asset Value | Liability | Monthly Payment | Monthly Income | +/- Cash Flow |
|------|-------------|-----------|-----------------|----------------|---------------|
|  | Duplex 210 Anywhere St $100,000 | $90,000 | $644.79 | $800 | +$164.21 |
|  | Car Payment | $10,000 | $350 | $0 | -$350 |
|  | Credit Card | $8,000 | $150 | $0 | -$150 |
|  | Savings Account | $2,000 | $0 | $2 | +$2 |
|  |  |  |  |  |  |
|  |  |  |  |  |  |
|  |  |  |  |  |  |
|  |  |  |  |  |  |
|  |  |  |  |  |  |
|  |  |  |  |  |  |
|  |  |  |  |  |  |
|  |  |  |  |  |  |
|  |  |  |  |  |  |
|  |  |  |  |  |  |
|  |  |  |  |  |  |
|  |  |  |  |  |  |
|  |  |  |  |  |  |
|  |  |  |  |  |  |
|  |  |  |  |  |  |
|  |  |  |  |  |  |
|  |  |  |  |  |  |
|  |  |  |  |  |  |
|  |  |  |  |  |  |
|  |  |  |  |  |  |

**Have a Super Fantastic Life.** Have a Super Fantastic Life.

*If you see a bandwagon its too late.*

*James Goldsmith*

If you have a new car you bought for $30,000 yesterday you would list that as an asset. If you bought it with nothing down the liability will be $30,000. However the value will be only around $25,000 (Buying a brand new car never has and never will be a good investment).

If you just bought the big screen TV mentioned above, list it as an asset and for the value put Zero. Under liability put what is owed on it, and then the monthly payment amount. The reason you will put zero as an asset is because it has very little to no resale value.

Total up the value column and the liability column. Subtract the liability from the value. If this is a negative number you need to change your life NOW!

If it is a positive number, then you have things going in the right direction. But you will still want to have a goal of getting your liabilities to ZERO. We will work on changing your habits to make this happen.

To get liabilities to zero you will need to pay off your debt.

How? You may need to sell some items (like a second car) and downsize. Get an extra job to pay it off sooner. Ask the lender to reduce your rate, or cut expenses somewhere else to make more payments. You are not the federal government and cannot last long while running your financial life in the RED.

> There are lenders and investors who will give you money based on the deal, not your ability to repay or your credit.
>
> — unknown

# 11 — Spending Habits

Is it pain or pleasure? To become financially free there will be pain. Any time you change habits it will be difficult. Like the old saying goes: NO PAIN NO GAIN.

Life is all about habits. We all have habits. Some of us lay in bed when we wake up, some of us get up right away. Some of us smoke while others don't. Some are addicted to alcohol or drugs. Some exercise every day and some never have. Some make sure the toilet paper unrolls from the top down.

The point is we all have habits even if we don't think of them as such. Some habits are good some are bad. Changing a habit is not easy. No one said it would be. But to reach your financial goals and to become Financially Free you will need to change your bad financial habits.

I am always trying to lose weight. Most of the time I am on the "seefood" diet. (I See Food and eat it). I tell my wife to keep the junk food, cookies, candy, and chips in a separate area because if I see it I will eat it.

Changing my eating habits is hard and I continue to work at it.

*Nothing is so embarrassing as watching someone do something that you said couldn't be done.*

— B.C. Forbes

## SPENDING HABITS

Changing your financial habits won't be easy but it will be easier than changing your eating habits.

My daughter Sadie was having a great basketball year as a freshman for the Assumption Royals. In the opening tournament, The Cranberry Classic, she was named to the Junior Varsity All-Tournament Team. She played so well that they moved her up to the Varsity team. For the next four games, she was playing GREAT basketball. Then, at a game in Marathon, she went up for a rebound, got bumped, came down wrong and dislocated her kneecap. She laid there in pain until she was carried off by some of the coaches and myself. She had to create a new habit to be able to play basketball again. Lifting her leg weight daily and getting up at 5:30 a.m. to go to the Physical Therapy department to lift weights and strengthen her leg. She was VERY dedicated. Through hard work, she is back to playing and starting on the Varsity team as a junior. The Royals are undefeated and ranked #1 in the state at the time of writing this. She made her workout routine a habit. A good habit. This is what everyone needs to do with their financial habits.

The problem with habits is most of us don't even know we have them. A couple of years ago I got golf sandals for Christmas. I love golfing in them. After putting one day my wife said, "Do you know you lift your toes three times, every time before you putt?" I didn't realize this, but once she told me I realized this had become a habit of mine. Not that this is a good or bad habit it is just a habit I was not aware I had. Bad habits come easy. Good habits can take time, but with work and dedication they will make a positive difference in your life.

The first step is to be aware of your spending habits. You will do this by making a list of every penny you spend. Yes, EVERY PENNY and what it was spent on needs to be written down.

**Have a Super Fantastic Life.** Have a Super Fantastic Life.

*The Chinese use two brush strokes to write the word "crisis". One brush stroke stands for danger, the other for opportunity. In a crisis, be aware of the danger, but recognize the opportunity.*

*John F Kennedy*
*35th president of the United States of America*

When you get gas, write it down. If you buy a candy bar when you get gas, write it down separately. When you go shopping, itemize everything separately. Do this for 30 days, then look at all of your purchases to see where you could have saved money.

The reason you will want to write them down separately is so you can identify individual items on which you can save money. If you get gas for $59.71 plus a bag of chips for $3.29 and a bottle of Coke for $1.50, but just write down $64.50 for gas, you cannot see where to save the money. When you write it all down you can see you did not need the coke or the chips. Not buying these would save you $4.79. If you get gas once per week that is a savings of $249.08 per year.

I know it will not be easy but remember it is only for one month. When you go shopping for food and write down everything separately, you will be amazed at the stuff you buy that you do not need.

Trust me... none of us need a candy bar, especially a $1.00 one. We can all do without fast food, or buying unnecessary items at the grocery store. When shopping, make a list and STICK to it. Marketing is defined as: a philosophy based on thinking about the business in terms of customer needs and their satisfaction. The stores put the most profitable items at eye level. They also position impulse items at easy spaces, like by the cash register. Start looking at this when you shop and even make a game of it with your spouse and children if they are old enough. Ask them to find the highest priced item that the store is trying to promote and discuss how they are doing this. How is the item positioned? The marketing material used? The price (buy one get one free or buy one get one half off)? Making you and your family aware of this can help you all form good spending habits for life.

You will be amazed at the end of the month where you can save money and cut expenses. Once you have done

*The wealthy are not in the market, the wealthy control the market.*

— unknown

this you can then start planning for reaching and exceeding your financial goals. I am not saying you can NEVER have another candy bar, just making you aware of what you are spending money on. You can then plan and budget for items like a candy bar.

When I was growing up it was a treat to have a can of Jolly Good Soda on Saturday nights. Even though I can now have a soda whenever I want one, drinking water is much healthier and saves money. So having a soda only once per week becomes a treat for me, and I am healthier and save money in the process.

When you go to a restaurant and order an appetizer for $6.50, soda for $2.50, entree for $15.00, and dessert for $4.95, your total will be $28.95 plus tax $1.60 and tip $6.11, for a grand total of $36.66. You can save a lot by drinking water or not having an appetizer or desert (or splitting one). This will also save you on tax and tip. That is why you need to itemize everything on your worksheet.

Having credit cards and using them to go on "feel good" shopping binges is just like having a drug or alcohol habit. Unnecessary or habitual credit card use will get you deeper and deeper into financial trouble. What happens is you go to the store to get a gallon of milk, but you had a fight with your spouse and you see wine on sale. You say, "You know what? I deserve to have a bottle of wine after the way I was just treated plus some cheese, crackers, and of course chocolate." It is easy to buy all this on your credit card. If you go into the store with just $5.00 then you cannot spend more than $5.00. As stated earlier the milk in most stores is positioned the farthest away from the front doors as possible. Why? Because the store managers want you to walk past other items they hope you will buy.

You will also want to shop for the best prices, coupons, etc. Just the other night my wife and I went out to dinner with my stepdaughter and her boyfriend. My wife had a

**Have a Super Fantastic Life.**

*The truth is, nobody's interested in the commodity. People buy feelings.*

*— unknown*

**SPENDING HABITS** 133

$5.00 coupon for the place we went out to dinner. We saved $5.00 just like that.

Make a list before you go shopping and stick to this list. Search the internet for coupons for items you are going to be purchasing. We have saved over $200 a month for our family of four.

Have a Super Fantastic Life. Have a Super Fantastic Life.

> The great thing about real estate is you can use a property that you have acquired to purchase more property or put profits in your pocket, without even having to sell your initial investment.
>
> — unknown

# 12 Financial Goals and Retirement Planning

My sister once asked me for advice on a crop she and her husband were looking at planting. I asked what her goals were, and she said "What do you mean?" I said, "When do you plan on retiring? When does your husband plan on retiring?" She said they had never really talked about it. I told her she and her husband need to meet with a financial planner to help them set goals before they did anything. I said, "You need to know where you are going so you know when you get there."

What are your financial goals?

What do you want to do when you retire?

Only you and your spouse can answer these questions.

I will share with you our goals.

We are on track to be totally debt free before 59. That means having everything we own paid off, including our house, condo and all commercial and rental properties.

Our condo in Mexico is paid in full, and our house is paid in full twice. We bought it, remodeled it, and paid it off. Then when we bought the condo in Mexico it was much cheaper to get a loan on our house and use the money for the condo. So now our house is paid off for the second time.

**Have a Super Fantastic Life.**

## Mike's Partial Bucket List

Own a Packer-yellow Corvette convertible
Buy my wife a diamond necklace
Travel to all 50 states
Golf the top 100 golf courses in the world
Visit Switzerland, Spain, Italy, Poland, Australia
Take a cruise with my wife and kids for our 25th anniversary
Cruise the Panama Canal
Have dinner with the President
Take my brother and sisters to Las Vegas
Golf Augusta National

We are planning on building a new home. To do this, we will have a loan on our house for the third time. The plan is to have it paid off in five years or less, which will still leave us debt free at the age of 59. If we continue to own everything we own now, we should have a significant annual cash flow. This will leave us in a very good financial position.

Our plan is to be able to retire in 2019 or 2020. While I don't believe I will ever totally retire, our plan is to be in a position to do so at that time.

My wife and I also plan on seeing the world. We love to travel together and we keep adding things we want to do and places we want to go to our Bucket List.

So many people are in fear of retirement because of their failure to plan for it. My wife and I are not wishing the next eight to nine years of our lives away. We discuss and make plans for our future. We continue to enjoy the journey.

I cannot emphasize enough how important it is to have goals, and to have those goals IN WRITING. Shout your goals to the world. There is extensive research on how having goals, and having them in writing, compared to no goals makes a difference in an individual's success. Most people plan their vacations more than their life. Plan your life and you will have a GREAT one!

**Have a Super Fantastic Life.** Have a Super Fantastic Life.

*If cash is king then real estate flipping is your throne.*

— unknown

# 13

## Just Ask...

You never know what you will get by just asking. I am writing this chapter on a flight coming back home from the National Realtor Convention in New Orleans. I left my hotel at 4:30 a.m. for my 6:30 a.m. flight. I tried to change my seat but noticed on the touch screens that all the seats where full. At the gate I asked if they were looking for volunteers to give up their seats and the agent said they were. I asked what they were offering and he said a $400 travel voucher for anywhere in the world. You must book within 1 year. I asked if they were giving any food vouchers and he said he could give one for breakfast.

I waited for the plane to board and they did need my seat. I patiently waited for James to finish with the passengers that could not get a seat. Because of my patience and understanding he gave me two meal vouchers: one for breakfast and one for dinner. I also asked for a pass to the elite club. He could not give me one, but it did not hurt to ask.

My wife usually doesn't like to take flight bumps and neither do I. But the airport had free wireless internet, and I knew I would only be getting back about four hours later by taking the bump. I would have gone to my office to work, but I did my work at the airport and got home for dinner

**Have a Super Fantastic Life.** Have a Super Fantastic Life.

*The best time to do something worthwhile and newsworthy is between yesterday and tomorrow.*

*RJS*

at the same time I would have gotten home if I went on the earlier flight. Plus, now I had a free flight coming. When a buddy of mine booked a trip out West, he paid me $350 for the $400 voucher. A win/win, he saved $50, I got the cash.

While I am not suggesting you ask McDonald's if they will give you a dollar off on a Big Mac meal, I am suggesting that you look at the situation and when it warrants asking, do it in a nice, professional manner.

When I arrived at the hotel for the convention, my air conditioning was not working. I informed the hotel and then went out to dinner with my nephew. When I came back around 10:30 p.m. it was still not working. They said it would be repaired the next day. The next morning before I left I talked to the front desk again. They said they were aware of it and it would be taken care of. I did not get back to my room until around 8 p.m. You guessed it, still not working. They brought up a portable unit, which worked okay, but not great. They never did get my air conditioning working.

The night before I left, I talked to the manager and explained what had happened. She checked the notes, apologized, and offered me a discount of one night free. I would have preferred the air conditioner to be working, but was satisfied with the refund.

Some people will not complain until they leave and expect all nights to be free. I know everyone makes mistakes and things happen. I was not trying to take advantage of the hotel, as I had informed them several times.

Always treat people with respect and always call them by their names.

When I bought my wife's engagement ring (a one carat diamond solitaire) I asked the jeweler two things:

1. If she says NO, will you give me a refund or a store credit? He agreed to give me a refund.

**Have a Super Fantastic Life.**

*There is no limit to what can be accomplished if no one cares who gets the credit. You are in a position to unleash greatness. Delegate not just the unpleasant jobs, and watch what can be done.*

*unknown*

This was important to me as I did not want to have a $6000 credit at a jewelry store to remind me that the girl of my dreams said NO.

2. I asked if he would give me a discount for paying cash over a credit card. Merchants pay a fee to the credit card companies on all sales. He had to pay 5%. I saved $300 by paying in cash.

Speaking of diamonds, for our 10th anniversary (by the way, she said yes and we have been happily married for over 15 years) I wanted to buy my wife a pair of diamond earrings. I wanted solitaires and the total weight to be one carat or more. The jewelry store had a pair I thought she would love. The problem was they were on sale for $3100 and the most I wanted to spend was $2500. Knowing jewelry has a very large markup, I talked to the owner and said I thought the earrings were beautiful but my budget was $2500. She went to look at her invoice, came back and said okay. I then asked her, "If I pay the $2500 in $100 bills instead of a credit card would you discount the fee that you normally pay to your credit card company?" I pulled out my wallet and paid in cash, less a 5% discount (saving another $125 just by asking.)

When my wife and I furnished our house, we went to a large furniture company that was always offering "buy now, pay later." It only took us about two hours to find all the furniture for our living room, bedroom, dining room, and kitchen that we thought would look great. Since I do construction work I asked if they had a contractor's discount. He went to his manager and gave us 5% off the sales price. I then asked him if there would be a discount if we paid for it all now as compared to paying in 12 months. We got another 10% discount. In all, just by asking and waiting, we saved $1500.

**Have a Super Fantastic Life.**

*To know what is right and not do it is as bad as doing it wrong.*

*— unknown*

I later learned the best question you can ever ask when you are buying a large item (over $500):

IS THAT THE BEST YOU CAN DO?

This has saved me thousands of dollars so far and will save me thousands more in the future.

Of course there have been times when they say "No," but there have been many times when they say "No," but offer free delivery or free extended warranty, which still saves me money.

My wife often reminds me of the phrase "Is that the best you can do." Although she very seldom will use it as she dislikes asking for discounts, she does like to remind me.

I went to take a second look at a manufactured home that was for sale. The sellers were very motivated. Before I went inside, my wife reminded me about "is that the best you can do?" I took her advice, and after I asked I just shut up and waited. It seemed like a minute went by (but was probably only 10 long seconds) before they looked at each other and said they would take $5000 (which was $1500 less than I was willing to pay). I had to turn my head and bite my cheek. I then said I would take it. I know if I would have come back with "can you do any better" I am sure I would have saved another $500.

You can call me cheap, but I call myself smart when it comes to money.

Just by asking, the following occurred:

I am in my 16th year of *Monday Morning Quarterback*. It is a radio show about the Green Bay Packers that I host. I was lucky to go to the Super Bowl in January of 1997. The Packers beat the Patriots. My best friend Kory had two tickets. We went with two other buddies and had a fantastic time. Before we left, I called up the local newspaper to see if they were interested in doing an article about the Super

> *Winners are those people who make a habit of doing things losers are uncomfortable doing.*
>
> — Jack Canfield

Bowl. They said yes and asked if they could come right over. The next day on the front page of the paper was an article: *Local Realtor Going to the Super Bowl*. You can't buy advertising like that. They then asked if I would be willing to give daily reports, and of course I said "Yes!" After thinking about it, I called the local radio station and talked to their sports manager. They were excited and asked me to call in twice daily and give reports. Again all this advertising for free. I was in the local newspaper and on the radio every day for seven days. All great advertising and all for free.

A couple weeks after the Super Bowl, I called Terry Stake, the sports manager at WFHR, and suggested doing a radio show every Monday after Packer games. For 16 years I've had the privilege of hosting this show. It has allowed me to get press passes for the Packers, be in the Press Box, on the field before and after the game, in the interview room, locker room, and more. I have asked questions of the head coaches, Brett Favre, Aaron Rogers, and others. I was on the field for Brett Favre's 200th straight start for the Packers. It was a Monday night game. At the end of the game when Favre blew a kiss to his wife, I was about 6 feet away from him. The cameras were on him and several people called me the next day, "Hey Zurf was that you on Monday night football?" Not bad for just asking.

Doing the football program then gave me the idea to do another show, *Real Estate 101*, during the off-season. This will be my fourth successful year of doing this show. It is a call-in show about real estate, and I have different guests and different subjects related to real estate every week. Both *Monday Morning Quarterback* and *Real Estate 101* have made my name prominent in the community when people think of Real Estate and the Green Bay Packers.

All of this happened because I JUST ASKED!!!

**Have a Super Fantastic Life.**

*Once you taste the action of the playing field, you will never again be content to sit in the bleachers!*

*unknown*

## Rental Cars

When I get a rental car, I always try to call the person that assigns the car by their first name. Once, my wife and I were in San Francisco for a real estate convention with our friends, John and Patty. We were going to Napa Valley for two days and rented a car. I had reserved a midsized car. When I went to pick it up I called Diane by her name and told her that the sweater she had on looked very nice. She smiled and thanked me. I then told her the Jag behind her would work just fine. She laughed and continued to fill out the paper work. When she was done she handed me the keys to the Jaguar. What a ride!!! For the same cost as the midsize I rented. It's amazing what you get out of life by JUST ASKING!!

**Have a Super Fantastic Life.** Have a Super Fantastic Life.

*Don't follow the crowd off the cliff.*

— unknown

# 14 Real Estate Investments

Investing in real estate is great because you can get rich using OPM: Other People's Money.

Using other people's money is a great way to make money in real estate, and if you do your homework, it can be very safe. However, like most sound investments, real estate profit happens slowly, not overnight.

The great thing about real estate is you can buy with 20% or less down. In some cases, even in this tough real estate market, you can start with no money down.

One way to buy with no money down is with bank owned, or REO (Real Estate Owned), properties.

REO are typically foreclosed properties that a bank now owns. There are times when a bank will take a deed in lieu of foreclosure. What this means is the bank will allow the owner of the property to sign the deed over to the bank and then just walk away. This process can save the bank money as the process to foreclose is very time consuming and costly. They lose money on taxes, insurance, attorney fees, lost interest, and deteriorating vacant property. Remember, banks DO NOT want to own real estate, they make their money by lending money. A great way to buy investment properties is to talk to your local banks and find out

*It's never to soon but it will soon be to late.*
*— unknown*

who the contact is for their REO properties. This works best with locally owned banks as you can get to know this person on a personal basis. Look at these homes, and when you find one that you think will work, talk to the bank and see what kind of deal they will give you. Sometimes they will sell you the property with no money down and a great rate. If you need money to fix it up, just ASK. Always remember to ask, "IS THAT THE BEST YOU CAN DO?"

I've bought several REO Properties in my life. With all of them the bank has agreed to loan me the full amount, usually at a low interest rate. They have also loaned me extra money to rehab the property.

I bought two different four-unit apartment buildings from a bank years ago. They loaned me the full amount at a low fixed interest rate. After we agreed on terms, I was allowed inside to inspect the properties. They were in surprisingly good shape. The only major problem was it was winter and the windows were old aluminum windows, so they had a buildup of frost on the inside. I took a proactive approach and got an estimate to replace all the windows. The cost was over $25,000. I went back to the bank, informed them of the problem and the bank offered to raise the price $10,000 and pay for the entire cost of new windows. We did the deal under those terms. Today, with the knowledge I now have, I am confident I could have negotiated for them to pay the entire cost of the new windows without an increase in sales price.

For many of you that are reading this book, you may say, "Yeah sure, you have a history with these banks." Let me tell you a little about my history. My mother loaned me the money for the first house I bought. I was 20 years old at the time. I paid $7500 and borrowed $8000 from my mother. Borrowing money from family and friends is not normally a good idea, and I don't recommend it. My mother and I had a special relationship. We put our agreement in writ-

*I hear babies crying, I watch them grow. They'll learn much more, than I'll ever know, and I think to myself, what a wonderful world.*

— Louis Armstrong

ing with me paying her a better interest rate than she was getting from savings at the bank, and saving me a little on what I would have to pay to get a bank loan. The house was trashed, but in good structural condition. I bought it, fixed it up, and lived in it. I had a buddy of mine move in with me and pay rent, which covered three quarters of the payment. I later rented it out and made a profit of over $50 a month. I know that is not a lot, but minimum wage at the time was $2.35 per hour. A couple years later I sold the house for $15,000, a profit of over $5000 more than what I had stuck into it.

The third and fourth house I bought was from a local bank. I had a savings account with them and they knew I had bought two other rental units. They loaned me the full amount and money to rehab them. This was when fixed interest rates were at 18%. Variable rates were at 12% and they could go up 1% every six months. I was able to get a great deal (at the time): my interest rate was fixed for five years at 12%. I bought both houses with no money down, fixed them up, and turned a profit of $200 per month, $100 per unit.

Owning real estate is not for everyone. There are problems and hassles but it has put me in a position to be financially set for the rest of my life.

**Have a Super Fantastic Life.** Have a Super Fantastic Life.

That's leverage. That dictionary defines leverage as "the use of a small initial investment, credit or borrowed funds to gain a high return on the initial investment."

unknown

**REAL ESTATE INVESTMENTS**     **157**

Connect all the dots with only 4 lines without taking your pencil off the paper

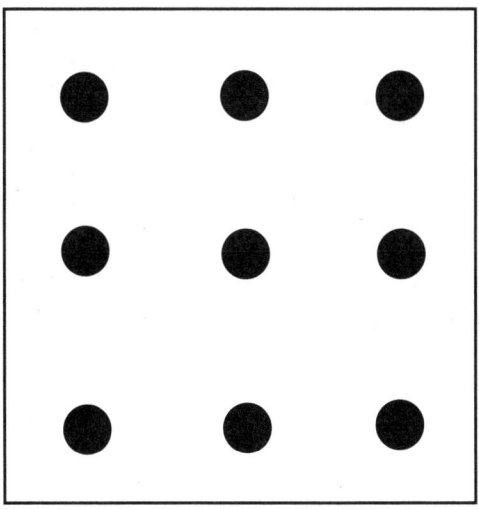

Try this exercise before turning the page.

**Have a Super Fantastic Life.** Have a Super Fantastic Life.

*Real state is the basis of all wealth. The more people the government has owning houses, the more it helps the government, so the more taxes they get.*

*unknown*

**REAL ESTATE INVESTMENTS**     **159**

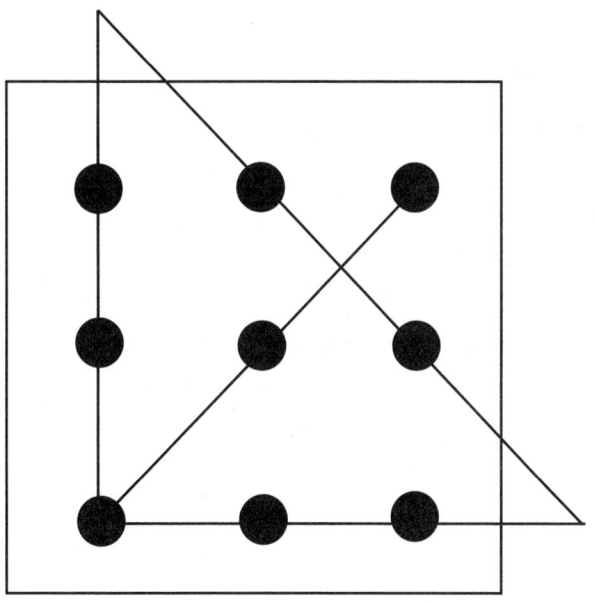

Think Outside the Box!

**Have a Super Fantastic Life.** Have a Super Fantastic Life.

*The wealthy are not in the market – the wealthy control the market.*

*unknown*

### The one that got away.

Years later, another bank had a log home on the back waters of the Wisconsin River for sale. They sent it out to investors for sale to the highest bidder. I looked at the home and determined it was in above average condition. I felt I would have to stick between $2000-$5000 to have the home in great shape. I bid $142,000 cash for it. The bank sold it to another investor for $144,000 with the bank financing the entire amount at a fixed rate of 4%. (This is one of the reasons I have a baseball bat with the boot attached in my office, to kick myself in the ass). At the time I was borrowing money at 6%. I could have offered to pay $150,000 with the bank financing at 4% and been better off. I now usually will give multiple offers in situations like that. The first is cash, the second one with bank financing, and the third with bank financing more than the full amount for improvements. THINK OUTSIDE THE BOX. I later learned that the investor had rented it out for a positive cash flow and ended up selling the home to the renter for a $100,000 profit. Cha-Ching! (For the other guy, not me.)

### The price of a Harvard education in a day.

There was a manufactured home park that was going to be sold at sheriff sale. I had talked to the bank and found out the owner owed the bank over $1,500,000. The bank was aware the property was not worth anywhere near this. I got busy, and before you know it the day of the sheriff sale arrived. I had my assistant call the bank's attorney two days before the sheriff sale to find out the bank bid. They told her $400,000, and there was also $100,000 in back taxes owed. I was excited and went to the sheriff sale looking to buy this property. I ran up to the sale just before it was going to start. There was the deputy that conducted the sale, another man that I had seen at these sales before but never bought any properties, and a man in a suit that I thought was the attorney for the bank. The deputy got to

*If you want your dreams to come true, don't oversleep.*

— American Proverb

**Have a Super Fantastic Life.**

the property and went over the legal description and all the particulars that needed to be stated. She started to say the opening bid when the man in the suit interrupted her. He said his name and that he was the attorney for a newly formed company that bought the mortgage from the bank yesterday and their bid was $700,000. It was like someone walked up to me and kicked me in the guts. I was sick to my stomach. What happened???

I waited until the sale was over and talked to the attorney. I told him I was interested in buying the property and got his information and the new owner's information. I later talked to the new owner, who said the bank did not want to get the property back so he bought the mortgage from them for $400,000. I then negotiated with the new owner, and we agreed that I would buy the property for $700,000 with all the property taxes paid in full. This man made a $200,000 profit with VERY little work and in around just 30 days. I got an expensive education. I worked very hard fixing the property up over the next 4 years, took NO money out and sold it for a $200,000 profit. He did very little work for 30 days and made the same. The cost of education is not cheap!

Another way to buy with no money down is on a land contract. A land contract is where the seller acts as the bank. The seller sells the property they own to you on a land contract. For example: the sale price is $100,000 and you have 10% down. The seller takes the $10,000 down payment from you and then you pay the balance of $90,000 on terms agreed to between you and the seller. Usually a land contract has a balloon payment. In a standard bank-financed loan you would have a full term loan, like a 15 or 30-year mortgage. This means if you have a 15-year mortgage and make all the scheduled payments, you will own your home free and clear in 15 years. With a land contract and a balloon payment, the seller may allow you to amortize the loan over 30 years. The balloon payment means

*Let go of the negatives in your life.*

*unknown*

you will have to pay the balance at a predetermined time, such as five years. Having the 30-year amortization will lower your payments to an affordable amount. For example, a $100,000 sale with 10% down and an interest rate of 6% over 30 years: your monthly payment will be $539.60. After five years your balloon payment will be $83,748.92. If you can find a seller with a vacant home you may be able to convince them to sell to you on a land contract.

Sometimes sellers, due to financing, are not willing to negotiate much on price. But price is only one aspect. Terms are just as important. I once bought a manufactured home park in which the seller wanted to finance a large portion of the sale. They did not want to get all the cash so they could avoid the high taxes associated with the large cash payment. It was complicated because the seller was selling all the stock in the company that owned the real estate. He was set on a price of $900,000. Because of the stock purchase I would have only a limited amount of time to depreciate the improvements. In our last meeting with the sellers, my accountant told us that with the used up depreciation, the most the property was worth was $750,000. The seller stormed out saying the deal was off. I was able to catch him and asked him to give me a minute. I then met in private with my accountant.

I said, "He is set on getting $900,000, I know this is a great property for me. He wants 7.5% interest on the $650,000 mortgage he will give back to me. What if I give him the $900,000 and get the loan at 6%?" My accountant said it was better but we would still be about $75,000 short.

I then said, "What if the seller would raise rents by $10 per month? That would be an extra $500 per month cash flow." He said it would be tight but would work.

I sat back down with a still-fuming seller. I told him I would be willing to pay him the $900,000 that he wanted. He was happy about that. I then told him I would need two

*Profit is not a dirty word.*

*— Mike Zurfluh*

things from him. 1: The interest rate would be 6% fixed for 10 years. 2: He would have to raise the rents $20 per month. The rents had not been raised in three years. He said I will agree to the 6%, but I will not raise the rents before closing, He said he would let me raise the rents and have them take effect the day of closing, as he did not want to look like the bad guy to his tenants. This all happened over 10 years ago. I still own this property and will have it paid off in full in less than 8 years. It will then be a cash cow. CHA-CHING!!!

Land contracts can work well for both the buyer and the seller. I recently sold a house that I had bought and fixed up. With the financing and real estate market the way it is, I agreed to sell the rehabbed house for full price at 7% interest, 30 year amortization with a balloon payment in three years, and $10,000 down payment. This creates a win/win. I have the property occupied, and they were able to buy a house even though they could not get financing at the time as her husband just started a new job. I now have a cash flow of approximately $250 per month over what my payments are plus have the $10,000 they put down.

Whether you are buying or selling, find out what the other party's goals or plans are for the money/property. Then look for a way to make a win/win situation.

HELP THEM REACH THEIR GOALS and profit at the same time.

When you are thinking about buying a home to live in or about buying rental property, a great way to start is with a duplex. I highly recommend side-by-side duplexes. In most cases you can have the tenant on the other side make your mortgage payments, or at least three quarters of it.

I am currently working with an investor that is looking to sell two side-by-side duplexes. He wants a price that is fair in the local market. 10 years ago I would have bought them at the asking price (even in the current real estate

*Love what you do!*

*unknown*

market). But with the position I am in now, I am only looking for great deals. My point is, the purchase would be a good deal for a new investor. The way I would approach the deal is to give him his asking price, but have him finance the sale with a low interest land contract. For both duplexes, which are both side-by-side and right next to each other, he wants to net at least $170,000. I would try to convince him to accept a $5000 down payment with a fixed interest rate at 3% or 4% amortized over 30 years, with a balloon payment in five years. As stated earlier, a balloon payment means the balance owed to the seller will need to be paid in full in five years (or otherwise specified), or the seller can reclaim the property. The payment on this at 3% would be $695.65 per month, taxes of about $400 per month and insurance of around $100 per month. Total monthly payment with PITI is $1198.65. For this example we'll make it an even $1200 per month. The rent is $500 per side, total of $2000. This would be a cash flow of $800 per month.

In five years most banks will not want to finance more than 75% of the property value. If you pay the extra $800 you are receiving in rent per month that would be an extra $48,000 you would have paid in five years off the principle. That means if you paid $175,000 for the two duplexes in five years you would owe $175,000 less the $48,000 = $127,000. You would also be paying down $19,762.71 in principle over the five years of the loan, leaving you owing only $107,237.39. This would be over 39% down from the original price you paid.

You would definitely be in a position to refinance in five years. But hold on. In four and a half years I would call the seller. I would make sure he/she was getting all my payments on time. I would ask if they would like to extend the land contract. Be quiet after you ask this question. If they say "No," then say, "I can understand that, I was not sure what your plans were to do with the money. I just thought if the interest rate was better than you can get wherever

**Have a Super Fantastic Life.** Have a Super Fantastic Life.

When is the best time to buy anything? When it's on sale! I make tons of money in so-called depressed markets because I get everything so deeply discounted. Then what do I do? I fix it up, making the cleanest and newest-looking house on the block and I sell it for less than anyone else in the neighborhood.

                                                    unknown

you were planning on investing it, you may want to keep getting it from me. As you know, I have never missed a payment and your investment is safe being backed up by the two duplexes."

This may get them to rethink and agree to extend the land contract. It may be at a higher rate of interest, but if it is lower than you can get from a bank, you still create a win/win situation. Keep in mind if you are paying the total rent of $2000 each month, this does not allow for vacancies and repairs. However if you pay $2052.68 per month you would have the duplexes paid off in eight years. Then you will have some serious cash flow every month. This would mean you would be paying an extra $400 per month for your side, but look at the position it puts you in.

This illustration also does not account for any rent increases. I usually will raise rents a minimum of 1% per year. I have talked to other investors and they say they leave rents the same and then every five years if they have the same renter will increase the rent $10 or $25. They lose out on a lot of money. $500 at 1% per year is:

1st year $500 x 101% = $505 per unit = $60 per unit
2nd year $505 x 101% = $510.05 =$120.60
3rd year $510.05 x 101% =$515.15 =$181.80
4th year $515.15 x 101% =$520.30 =$243.60
5th year $520.30 x 101% = $525.50 = $306.00

TOTAL AFTER FIVE YEARS IS $912.00

Some of you are saying, "What's the difference? If I just wait five years and raise it $25 I will be at $525 anyway." The difference is in five years you will have collected an additional $912. The other reason is I have never lost a renter over a 1% increase. Raise rents 5% one time and you will lose renters.

**Have a Super Fantastic Life.** Have a Super Fantastic Life.

*See life through the windshield, not the rear-view mirror.*

*unknown*

There are hassles with owning real estate as there are hassles with most things in life. Renters not paying rent on time (or not paying at all), damage to property, vacant units, and more. But let me tell you from personal experience there is no better way to create wealth and passive income than residential rental properties. Real estate can lead to financial freedom for the rest of your life. Remember: everyone needs a place to live.

**Have a Super Fantastic Life.**

*I'm not frightened of competition, because it can only make you better.*

*unknown*

# 15   Kids/ Education

I can still remember the day my first daughter was born, Sadie Ramona Zurfluh. My wife's due date was June 23. We had planned the baptism to be on the Fourth of July. During the last check-up she had with her doctor, he said that if she had not had the baby by July 6 that he would induce her. I said we have a little problem. We have the baptism planned for the Fourth. He was leaving for vacation on June 30. My wife was induced on June 28 at around 8 a.m. The contractions started to get stronger around 11:45 a.m. At around 12:20, as I was standing by my wife's side, the nurse said "Mike, come here." I thought I heard my wife groan "move and you're dead," so I stayed right where I was. A couple of seconds later the nurse said "Mike, come here NOW!" When I moved to the end of the bed I could see our baby starting to come out. My right foot FRPM (foot revolutions per minute) were at about 1000. Sadie Ramona was born at 12:22 p.m. Along with the birth of my second daughter, Macie Rita, it was the most amazing experience in my life. Yes, I got to cut the cord both times. From that moment on my two daughters have been the most important thing in my life. They bring me unimaginable joy, worry, and every other emotion in between. I would die for them. (I do have to agree with a statement I heard long ago.

**Have a Super Fantastic Life.**

*Opportunity always looks bigger going than coming.*

*unknown*

## KIDS/ EDUCATION

If men had to give birth, the human race would cease to exist. My wife did a great job during the delivery, but I can only imagine the pain she was going through at the time. Thanks Honey!)

The worry never stops and I am sure it never will. Not only about their well being, their health and happiness, but also for their financial future. My wife and I talk to them both about money and how to plan for their future.

We both believe in not giving our kids everything. Some, including me, might say they are both spoiled. But I will also tell you they have to work to pay for their cell phones and many other things in their lives. Our plan is to have them pay for their own college, help them get jobs and plan for the rest of their lives. In doing this we believe we have instilled many good attributes in both of them.

I believe that giving your kids everything is not doing them any favors for the future. Money is taboo for many families, but should be talked about on a regular basis. Everyone needs to know and understand who is responsible for money and how.

### College

One area that can get you the same results at a lower cost is when you are choosing a college with/for your children. Will choosing an expensive college for your undergraduate degree give you the same results as choosing the local community college? While there is no doubt having a degree from an Ivy League College will open some doors, I believe an individual's personality is more important. But if you or your child are set on an expensive college, there are many options. College scholarships are the first place to start. If you do not have success in getting a scholarship you may want to go to a local/technical college to complete the basics. This can save you considerably on the first two years of college. The credits can then transfer to a four-year college to finish the degree.

**Have a Super Fantastic Life.** Have a Super Fantastic Life.

What is enthusiasm? It comes from two Greek words "en" and "theos" which simply means: "God within!" We should all be in the enthusiastic people business! Build your people and your people will build your business.

unknown

You could get a job that pays for your college education. There are many companies that will pay to educate you. Most of the time they will pay for your tuition and books as long as you get a B average or better. You will have to do this on your own time, but can get a degree for free. Yes, it will take you longer, but if dedicated, you can finish in five to six years, all with no cost to you and while earning a full time wage to boot.

Joining the military is another way to pay for college. Most branches of our military will pay for all or most of a college degree if you serve for four years or more.

There are many ways to get a college degree without substantial debt when you graduate.

I recently met with a couple who wanted me to buy their home from them. My van has signage that says, "I Buy Houses," so I often get calls like this. When I arrived at the house, I started talking to them about the property and what they thought it was worth, and what they needed in their pocket. I found out they had purchased the home over 30 years ago for $25,000. They had done minimal improvements over the years. Their current debt on the house was $250,000. Considering the market, the property was now valued at $150,000. How can this happen? They told me they had continued to refinance the house as it appreciated in value. With the current economic situation, they both found themselves out of work. At a time when they should be closing in on retirement, they had a huge mortgage payment and were on the verge of bankruptcy. I won't get into how banks could let this happen, but wow! Don't let this happen to you! I am not sure what they did with the money that they pulled out of their home equity every time they refinanced, but I know they didn't put it back into the house. My assumption is they bought "stuff" with it that they no longer use, need, or probably have anymore. Had they kept the original 30-year mortgage, they would be in

**Have a Super Fantastic Life.**

*Talk to your kids about money. A lot.*

*— Mike Zurfluh*

a much better position to handle their job losses and probably be in a position to retire.

Paying off your credit card debt with a home equity loan is not the smart thing to do. People do this and then a couple of years later they have the credit cards all maxed out again. Then the problem is they owe more on their house than they did two years ago.

Use your house not as an asset to buy things but as an asset to acquire more wealth. When you get a raise, don't just put it in your checking account and spend it. Pay it towards the principle on your house, or pay off other debt. Think of it this way, assuming you have no other debt except for your house payment: If you have a 30 year loan on your house that is $1000 per month you can pay it off in 15 years instead of 30. If you took out the loan when you were 30 years old, you will be debt free by 45. Then if you save the $1000 per month you will have 180 months x $1000 = $180,000 at age 60. If you invest this at 7% interest that will turn into $316,962.30.

Talk to your kids about money when they are young. It will make them more responsible with money when they are teenagers and adults. Teaching your children to have good financial habits will give them futures to enjoy instead of fear. Most people spend what they make. Teach your children how to pay off any debt they have, save money and budget to spend some of their money for fun.

Rather than give our kids an allowance, we have a weekly sheet for them to fill out to earn their spending/ saving money. See a sample on the next page.

**Have a Super Fantastic Life.** Have a Super Fantastic Life.

*Believe and Succeed: Courage does not always roar. Sometimes, it is the quiet voice at the end of the day saying, "I will try again tomorrow."*

*— unknown*

## KIDS/ EDUCATION

| Date: _____  Activity | $$$$ | Mon | Tues | Wed | Thurs | Fri | Sat | Sun | Total |
|---|---|---|---|---|---|---|---|---|---|
| Make bed/ pick up | $0.50 | | | | | | | | |
| Exercise | $1.00 | | | | | | | | |
| Dishwasher | $1.00 | | | | | | | | |
| Practice Piano | $0.50 | | | | | | | | |
| Practice Flute | $0.50 | | | | | | | | |
| Practice Trumpet | $0.50 | | | | | | | | |
| Practice Violin | $0.50 | | | | | | | | |
| Garbage | $1.00 | | | | | | | | |
| Recyclables | $0.50 | | | | | | | | |
| AR Goal | $1.00 | | | | | | | | |
| Exceed AR Goal | $2.00 | | | | | | | | |
| Load of laundry | $1.00 | | | | | | | | |
| Clean up after meal | $1.00 | | | | | | | | |
| Set table for meal | $0.50 | | | | | | | | |
| Miscellaneous | $0.50 | | | | | | | | |
|  |  | | | | | | | | |
| Leaving kitchen mess | -$1.00 | | | | | | | | |
| Room/Bed not done | -$1.00 | | | | | | | | |
| Disrespectful to folks | -$2.00 | | | | | | | | |
| Fighting with sister | -$1.00 | | | | | | | | |
| Leaving mess | -$1.00 | | | | | | | | |

**Have a Super Fantastic Life.** Have a Super Fantastic Life.

*All that is necessary for the triumph of evil is that good men do nothing.*

— Edmund Burke

**From The Wall Street Journal Sunday March 28, 2010:**

## Teach Your Children Well

- Spending money happens only after you earn it.
- When kids start asking parents to drive to the toy store to buy some plastic whatnot, it's time to consider an allowance.
- The size of an allowance shouldn't be so meager that your child is a pauper among peers, nor so generous that your child can easily afford all wants with little financial planning.
- Good grades are expected and help around the house is simply the price of family life.
- While 16 is generally the legal age of employment, encourage kids starting around age 13 to think of ways they can earn an income.
- Failure to balance the debit card/bank account monthly means losing access to the debit card for a week or more. Failure to repay an entire month's credit card means no use until the balance is paid off, plus one additional month.
- Only 50% of the money put into a piggybank can be taken out to buy something. At least half must remain inside the pig.
- You don't need to be wealthy to begin teaching your children about the stock market.
- One of the greatest gifts you can give your child is your own financial self-sufficiency when you're old.
- At some point, you have to tell your kids that the Bank of Mom & Dad is officially closed.

Parents and Kids:

Remember to TEACH YOUR CHILDREN WELL

**Have a Super Fantastic Life.** Have a Super Fantastic Life.

*Never give up: Go over, go under, go around, or go through. But never give up.*

*— unknown*

# 16

# Cash Is King

Having cash can make a big difference in getting the great deals in life. I have already shared some stories about how having money will get the customer better deals. But you will not get better deals on small items with cash. You will get the better deals on larger purchases.

When you are buying a house, if you are in a position to make a cash offer with a large earnest money payment, your offer may get accepted over another larger offer that has to get financed.

When you are looking to buy a car, especially a used car, if you show up with cash or your checkbook you are in a GREAT position to make a deal.

This is true for most large ticket items, especially used items. Most of these sellers are very motivated. They want to sell and they want to sell it NOW. You need to remember from earlier in this book: "Is that the best you can do?" Ask them if I pay you in full today, what is the best you can do?

Cash is also king when buying investment properties. Not only will it get you a good deal when buying, but it is also what will get you the loan at the best rates. What I mean is if the deal is good enough, the cash (loan) will find you. Banks are in the business of lending money, that is how they

*Remember who you wanted to be.*

*unknown*

make a profit. They want to lend money to owner-occupied properties or investment properties that have great CASH FLOW, meaning the property has an excellent rental history and there is sufficient cash to pay the maintenance expenses, taxes, insurance, and the monthly bank payment.

Remember to ask yourself: do you really need what you are looking to buy? Have walk-away power, if the deal is not good enough then walk away. What is the worst that will happen? You will not buy the item. You did not own it before you started to negotiate, so there is no loss.

A great way to not pay too much is to have a maximum price and stick to it.

I bought a work trailer from a construction company that was going out of business. When I went to look at the trailer the owner said he was selling his office and storage buildings. The storage buildings had 20 individual stalls. We talked price and I agreed to buy it for $110,000. I told him I would check with my bank and get back to him. I was sure I could get the loan, but told him if he found another buyer willing to pay more then to go ahead and sell it to them.

I checked with my bank a couple of days later and they were willing to loan me the money to do the deal. I called the seller back up and he said he already sold it. For CASH.

He told me the buyer wanted to talk to me about finding a renter for the office building. I called the buyer and we met at the building. I asked what he paid for it, thinking it was around $120,000. He said he paid $100,000. The seller was motivated and took the deal for $10,000 less than my offer. CASH is truly KING!!!

It's amazing what people will do for CASH.

Our town has about six loan businesses where you can get cash now for car titles, payday loans, etc. What you pay in interest is unbelievable. Why do people do this? Because they want the cash now.

**Have a Super Fantastic Life.** Have a Super Fantastic Life.

> *Your thoughts about your future are very important because you are going to spend the rest of your life there.*
>
> — unknown

I recently bought a weight set for my family. It was used, and valued at about $1000 new. It was still in very good condition. The owner was asking $550 for it. When I went to look at it I brought two $100 bills. I asked him what is the lowest he would take. He said $400. I then asked if that was the best he could do. He said he really wanted to sell it and he said he would take $300 for it. I asked him if he would take $200. He said NO. I then took the two $100 bills out of my wallet for him to see it. I said I have the cash today if you will take $200 for it. You guessed it, the weight set is now in my basement for my family and I to use for $200.

CASH IS KING, people will do some amazing things or sell at some amazing prices to get CASH now. Look at the interest rate the Cash Advance stores get and they all make a profit.

**Have a Super Fantastic Life.** Have a Super Fantastic Life.

*Time spent getting even would be better spent getting ahead.*

*— unknown*

# 17 Giving Back

The Bible says everyone should tithe.

Tithe: From old English: teogopa "tenth," is a one-tenth part of something, paid as a contribution to a religious organization or compulsory tax to government.

I know what most of you are thinking: I am trying to get out of debt and save money, there is not enough left to give back.

I disagree. You may not have the cash to give back, but you may be able to give back in the form of your time.

If you are making $10 per hour and you work 40 hours per week, 10% of that is $40 or four hours of your time.

Offer to clean your church. That may be four hours right there. Or be a greeter, lector, or usher at your church.

Be a coach for grade school or other levels. This can certainly be more than four hours of your time per week. Volunteer to help with the local Boy or Girl Scouts. If you play a musical instrument, volunteer at an assisted living or nursing home to play for a couple hours per week. Offer to read to children or senior citizens that can no longer read.

**Have a Super Fantastic Life.**

I often ask the question, "What would you say if I offered you 1,000 dollars for everything you could think of to feel grateful for?" My guess is, you would run out of paper to write your answers before you ran out of thoughts! That's because deep down, we all know that it's a miracle to be here. Life is a gift to be treasured. It was a gift when you were born, and it has been a gift ever since. Let's spread the message together, to create more kindness in this life, starting right now. You're worth it.

*unknown*

If you like to walk and be outdoors, then adopt a highway and keep it clean. A 35-minute walk per day will get you to your four hours, keep a highway clean and improve your health.

Shovel snow or mow the lawn of a neighbor who can't do it, or offer to do it for a fee that can be donated to a charity you both agree on.

Giving back is the right thing to do. It is the right thing to teach your children to do, and it is the right thing to have your children see you doing this. Get them involved with you, it will make for some lasting memories.

My daughter Macie would give all her money (and mine) away. Okay, maybe not all of it, but she is very emotional when there is a person asking for money. When we go to Mexico and go to the Melecon (Downtown Puerto Vallarta) we often run into people asking for money. I always give or I give the money to Macie to give to them. She sometimes asks why I don't give more. I explain that the first rule about money is to take care of your own money. If I give all my money away I can't help anyone and I will be in a bad financial situation myself and for our family.

**Have a Super Fantastic Life.** Have a Super Fantastic Life.

*What are we? We are Americans! It's not Ameri-I-can't! It's Amer-I-CAN!*

*— unknown*

# 18 Closing

In closing, getting to the position I have put myself in won't be easy. It's not supposed to be! For the last 10 years or so, I have kept track of the hours I work. I have averaged more than 55 hours per week for all 52 weeks in the year. Yes, I take vacations, and I only count the time I spend working while on vacation towards my total hours. If you work 40 hours per week, that works out to 2080 hours per year. If you have 6 weeks of vacation, and only work 40 hours the rest of the weeks of the year, you will average 35.4 hours per week, 1840.8 per year. It will be VERY hard to get ahead working only 35.4 hours per week. Putting in the extra time won't be easy at first, but once you form this good habit, it will become easy. Trust me, the rewards of financial freedom are worth the effort.

I just started reading fiction books. I like ones by Vince Flynn, and I just finished reading one by David Baldacci called *The Whole Truth*.

It is a novel about one of the richest men in the world trying to recreate the cold war to give him financial gain. A paragraph in the book states:

**Have a Super Fantastic Life.** Have a Super Fantastic Life.

*If 99% is good enough, then...*

- 2,000,000 documents will be lost by the IRS this year.
- 518,322 pieces of mail will be mishandled every hour.
- 22,000 checks will be drawn from the wrong account every hour.
- 12 babies will be given to the wrong parents every hour.
- 14,208 defective computers will be shipped this year.
- 107 incorrect medical procedures will be performed by the end of the day.

Good enough is not good enough. Only your best should be expected and accepted.

unknown

*Unless this country does a complete turnaround, in thirty years or less the Yanks will be finished. That's why I'm buying Euros, Yen, Yuan and Rupees, and looking to expand my clientele well beyond the land of the free, home of the brave. No one with that much debt is free and the home is mortgaged to the hilt. Still, they can enjoy it while it lasts, credit card their way for another couple decades anyway. Future generations will have to pay the piper and all hell will break loose when the bill comes due.*

I believe both citizens and our government have used credit in such a way that it will harm the greatest country in the world unless we change, and change NOW!

There will be pain but remember: NO PAIN, NO GAIN.

Take the steps NOW to change your financial habits and you will have the financial freedom to live a stress-free financial life.

If you are in debt now, take the steps in this book to get out of debt. If you own a home, work on getting it paid off as soon as possible. Your goal should be to become debt free and then to save and invest for your financial future.

Take care, God Bless you, and God Bless the United States of America.

Have a Super Fantastic Life!


Check out www.getzurf.com for more information or to book Zurf for your school, church or other events for free.

# About the Author

Mike Zurfluh was born in Nekoosa, WI on February 10, 1961, the youngest of eight children, to Ramona "Honey" Zurfluh and Harold Zurfluh.

Mike has been selling real estate since 1980. He and his wife, Celeste, have two children: Sadie Ramona and Macie Rita. Mike was the number one producer in his market from 1995 until 2011. He bought and sold over 200 homes during this time period. He also purchased six manufactured home parks, and at one time owned over 400 rental units. Today, Mike continues to list, buy, and sell real estate as well as speaking in schools and other businesses on The Truth About Money.

To contact Mike or get more information about speaking at your event, go to www.getzurf.com.